Y0-CLE-476

MY LIFE IN BITS 'N' PIECES

Also by Gene Key

A Bit of My Heart, Volumes 1, 2 and 3

My Life in Bits 'N' Pieces

Gene Key

Copyright © 2001 by Gene Key

All rights reserved. No part of this book may be reproduced or transmitted in any form or by any means, electronic or mechanical, including photocopying, recording, or by any information storage or retrieval system, without prior written permission from Koenisha Publications, except for the inclusion of quotations in a review.

The information contained within these pages is accurate to the author's best ability to verify the facts. Some discrepancies exist in the names of some of the ancestors listed on the historical pages, which have been maintained as recorded in the official and legal documents.

All Bible references are in the King James Version.

Library of Congress Control Number: 2001091580

Koenisha Publications
3196 – 53rd Street
Hamilton, MI 49419-9626
Phone or Fax: 616-751-4100
Email: koenisha@macatawa.org
Website: www.koenisha.com

I would like to dedicate this book to my children, all seven of them. They have made my life what it is. For without them, there would be no life or book.

I acknowledge their contribution, the pain they caused me and the great joy they have given me. But most of all I want to acknowledge and give thanks to my Lord for being with me and giving me the strength I needed to raise seven children alone, and cope with all the problems that came with them. He has been my health, my strength, my guide, and constant companion. To Him I give all the praise!

I thank Dr. Earl S. Rhind for his encouragement. He was the first person who ever suggested I write my thoughts on paper.

My thanks also, to my writing teacher, Sharolett Koenig, for all she taught me and for the many questions she answered for me.

IMPORTANT CHANGES OR EVENTS DURING MY LIFE

1921 – I was born to Bernie Bethel and Ruth Alice (Nixon) Underwood on July 28th.
Warren G. Harding was president.
1923 – President Harding died.
"Cal" Coolidge became president.
1924 – Billy Burke Underwood, my brother, was born.
1927 – Charles Lindbergh flew solo to France.
We had a big flood.
1928 – Herbert Hoover became president.
1929 – The stock market crashed, depression started.
1930 – Bryce Berniel Underwood, my brother, was born.
1931 – This brother died.
1932 – F. D. Roosevelt was elected president.
1933 – John Stanley Underwood, my brother, was born.
I saw my first 8-cylinder car. WOW!
1935 – One teacher changed my life. I also fell in love!
1936 – I graduated 8th grade.
The Hindenburg Airship was built.
1937 – Alice Elizabeth Underwood, my sister, was born.
Big Flood!
The Hindenburg crashed and burned as it was landing in New Jersey.
1940 – I married. He was a bigamist from Texas.
1941 – We were brought into the WWII.
The Bismarck was sunk.
1942 – We had food rationing stamps for sugar, shoes, gas, etc.

1943 – We used German P.O.W.s in our fields. What a joke!
1944 – President Roosevelt died.
1946 – I married my children's father.
1947 – My son, Roy Francis Key, was born.
1949 – My first daughter, Regina Gail, was born.
1951 – We came to Michigan for work.
1952 – We moved to Michigan to stay.
    Dwight D. Eisenhower became president.
1953 – My second son, Billy Jon, was born.
1955 – My second daughter, Starlyn Carol, was born.
1957 – My third daughter, Lee Ann Holly, was born.
1960 – My fourth daughter, Melodi Rae, was born.
    John F. Kennedy became president.
1963 – President Kennedy was killed in Texas.
1964 – My fifth daughter, Quaita Jahree, was born.
1965 – Americans were fighting in Vietnam.
1966 – My husband was killed in a car wreck in Arkansas.
1968 – Richard Nixon became president.
1969 – I bought a home in Holland, Michigan.
    My first son, Roy Francis, got married.
    My first grandchild, Terry Lynn, was born.
    Jimmy Carter became president.
1970 – My father died.
1973 – My mother died.
1974 – President Nixon resigned
    Gerald Ford became president.
1976 – My first daughter, Regina Gail, got married.
1977 – My second son, Billy Jon, got married.
    My grandson, Keri Jon, was born.
1978 – My second granddaughter, Kellie Raper, was born.

1979 – My second grandson, Joey Dean Graves, was born.
    Joey's mom and dad (Lee Ann Holly Key and Daryl Dean Graves) were married—little late.
    I bought my first and only new car, a silver Camaro.
1980 – Ronald Reagan became president.
1981 – My granddaughter, Teah Marie, was born.
1982 – My grandson, Shannon Raper, was born.
1983 – My youngest daughter, Quaita Jahree, got married.
    My grandson, Michael Dale Ver Hey, was born.
    My granddaughter, Michelle Lee Ann Graves, was born.
1984 – I retired from General Electric Company.
    My granddaughter, Ashley Ann Bridges was born.
1986 – My grandson, Chad Allen Ver Hey, was born.
1987 – My grandson, Joshua Paul Bridges, was born.
1988 – George Bush became president.
    My brother, Billy Burke, died of cancer.
1992 – Bill Clinton became president.

TABLE OF CONTENTS

Chronology	viii
Foreword	xv
Roots	xvi
Going a Long Way Back	1
Civil War Information	3
Francis Marion Underwood	
Jesse Underwood	5
My Great-Great-Grandfather	
Reverend Jesse's Life and Family	7
Fifth Generation	
Francis Marion Underwood—	17
My Great-Grandfather	
Fourth Generation	
John Henry Underwood—My Grandfather	23
Bernie Bethel Underwood—My father	33
Fay Imogene (Underwood) Key	37
Where I Came From	39
My Father, the Storyteller	43
My Son's Story About Dad	45
The Greatest Guy I Ever Knew	47
My Connection to Richard Nixon	55
Some Things I Remembered	61
My Birth	83
The Early Years	87
Pre-school Childhood	91
Elementary Years	95
Teenage Years	99
Young Adult Years	103
Flashbacks	113
Do You Believe in Angels?	117
The Good, The Bad and The Ugly	123
Earthquakes in Diverse Places	129

Racing Cars for Fun	133
The Gifts God Gives Us	139
Overly Confident, Sometimes	143
Thank God for Ears	147
Just Another Chapter in My Life	151
The Night I Was Saved	157
All Kids Are Not Bad	161
I Have a Question	163
The Importance of Time	165
A Trip to South Dakota	169
In Training	177
The Posture of Pain	181
One Large Regret	183
A Journey—Oases in My Desert	187
More About Oases	191
Unruly Thoughts and Things	195
A Place Where I Long to Go	197
I'll Share	199
Some Personal Observations	201
My Song	205
A Lot of Questions	207
My Aged Aunt's Story	209
To My First Grandchild	213
Father's Day	215
A Glorious Day	217
Hints of Despair	219
The Uninvited Guest	223
I Feel Special Today	227
Little Christopher	231
Looking to the Skies, But With Different Eyes	233
Let It Snow	237
Memorial Day 1996	241
Precious Memories	243
Keeper of the Flame	247

The Watchman	251
A Song of Thankfulness	253
I Love Things That Are Green	255
What Brought This On?	259
I Have a Confession	263
Mostly Fiction	267
Am I Allowed One Big Mistake?	269
Same Song—Second Verse	273
My Views on Retirement	281
A Great Controversy	285
For the Good Times—Some of the Time	291
Good Bye Jon-Jon	299
A True Story about My Eldest Son	301
To Advertise or Not	305
Looking Back, But Pressing Ahead	309
Tearing Down the Barn	315
Dual Personality	319
Rockyfellow Plaza	323
This Will Be a Quiet Day	327
The Rush and Hustle of Christmas	331
Slappy: My Pretty Girl	333
The Question	335
God Help Me Hear Your Voice	337
Comparisons	339
Lord, Help Me	340
Lord, I Need You!	341
My Request	342
Deep Calls to Deep	343
A Question of Worth	345
Some Things I Need to Know	347
Remembering Michael	349
The Modern Raven	351
A Lesson Well Learned	353
The Sadness in Colorado	355

Surprise! Surprise! 357
EPIMETHIUS: 359
   Something About Each of My Seven Children

FOREWORD

My reason for writing this is very simple. After I'm gone, I would like for my children's children's children to know who I was, where I came from and what contributions I have made to society, if any.

I went to a family reunion—my father's side of the family—a few years ago and found myself in a great crowd of my relatives that I had never even heard of. I felt I had missed a lot by not having known these people. So, I made a choice. In the days to come, if there is another reunion and my name is mentioned, I don't want my grandchildren to have to say, "Who was she?"

I think my life has had meaning. So far I've seen fourteen presidents, and who knows how many more I'll see. There have been five wars, many births, deaths, droughts, floods and The Great Depression to a great economy. I've fought my own battles, personal ones, and I even won a few of them!

I believe there is something in here for everyone. So, read on and enjoy!

ROOTS

Several years ago I was privileged to go to a family reunion of the Underwoods, which is my father's family. It was most intriguing, for there was an unknown cousin who had spent a lot of years tracing the background of this family. He furnished me with documents and other proofs of our connection. I was so excited to have records (not all of them complete) of at least six generations of my family.

I thought it might be interesting to include a bit of my past history along with my own remembrances of my life. So...
    1759 – William (Billy) Underwood was born.
    July 13, 1804 – Rev. Jesse Underwood was born.
    September 28, 1824 – Francis Marion Underwood was born.
    April 1866 – John Henry Underwood was born.
    October 2, 1895 – Bernie Bethel Underwood was born.
    July 28, 1921 – Fay Imogene (Gene) Underwood was born. ME!

I have included some Civil War records of some of the relatives who served in that war. Jesse Underwood had four sons who fought in that war, for the Union. One son fought for the Confederacy, and he is buried at Andersonville, Georgia. He died in the infamous Andersonville Prison. "Andersonville" was required reading when I was in school.

1/MY LIFE IN BITS 'N' PIECES

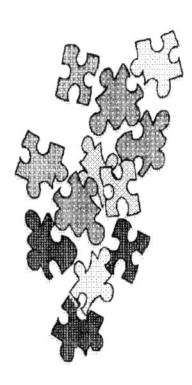

Going a Long Way Back

In 1938, Robert Taylor Underwood, a Confederate Civil War veteran, was living in Haywood County, North Carolina. He was ninety years old at the time. He dictated an outline of his Underwood ancestors to his second wife. Part of his outline stated, "My great-grandfather, Billie Underwood, was a Revolutionary War soldier. His children were as follows:
1. Jesse Underwood
2. Elijah Underwood
3. Fielding Underwood
4. Samuel Underwood
5. Enock Underwood
6. Bennett Underwood
7. Jimmie Underwood
8. Eliza Underwood

Seven of these brothers were Baptist preachers.

> NOTE: No documented proof exists at this time (3/81), but all evidence as stated above, and other evidence not listed in this outline, indicates that Jesse Underwood, born 1804, who married Mary

Ledbetter in 1822, is a son of Revolutionary War soldier William (Billie) Underwood (alias William Wedgbare). William was born in 1759 and enlisted from Culpepper County, Virginia in March 1780. He was in the Virginia Line commanded by Colonel Posey until 1783. He died March 4, 1852, at the age of ninety-two.

A William Underwood is listed in the 1820 Federal Census of Haywood County, North Carolina. His family consisted of the following:
 1 son under 10 years old
 2 sons 10-16 years old
 1 son 16-26 years old
 1 daughter under 10 years old
 A wife over 45 years old

William is listed as over 45 years old. Jesse Underwood was 16 years old when this census was taken, so it is very likely that this William was the father of Jesse.

A Felding Underwood is listed in the 1830-1870 Federal Census of Haywood County, North Carolina. He was living close to Jesse Underwood. It is believed Fielding and Jesse are brothers.

A pensioner by the name of William Underwood, age 80, is listed in the 1840 Federal Census of Haywood County, North Carolina. He was living in the household of Robert Brown. This is the same William Underwood that is listed in the 1820 census of Haywood County, North Carolina.

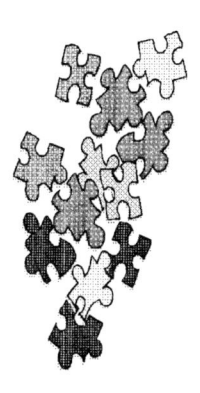

Civil War Information
Francis Marion Underwood

Born: September 28, 1824, in Haywood County, North Carolina
Married: To Susanna Vancil January 21, 1849, in Union County, Illinois
Died: December 18, 1901, in Greenway, Clay County, Arkansas
Enlisted: August 21, 1862, at Anna, Union County, Illinois for 3 years
Mustered in: September 11, 1862, Company "C" 109th Regiment Illinois Infantry Volunteer
Rank: Musician, Fifer (Flute)
Complexion – dark; Eyes – light; Hair – black; Height – 5 ft. 9 in.
Occupation: Farmer and Blacksmith
Deserted: December 20, 1862, at Holly Springs, Mississippi. Returned to regiment June 15, 1863, with loss of all pay and allowances during absence.
Transferred: From Illinois Infantry, Company "C", 109th to 11th Regiment, Illinois Infantry April 12, 1863.

Discharged: July 14, 1865, at Baton Rouge, Louisiana

Muster Roll Call, August 1864, sick in hospital at Vicksburg, Mississippi. While on duty at Mobile, Alabama, spring of 1865, was disabled by rheumatism, some loss of eyesight, nervous condition, catarrh of head and kidney disease.

Filed a Declaration for Invalid Pension January 14, 1890, with the above mentioned medical conditions. He received $6.00 per month. Filed for additional Invalid Pension May 30, 1891. He then received $12.00 per month until he died in 1901.

Most of the above information is taken from official records of the Civil War from the National Archives in Washington, DC.

Compiler:
Everett L. Hoebbel
Great-great-nephew of Francis M. Underwood
Reprinted here with permission

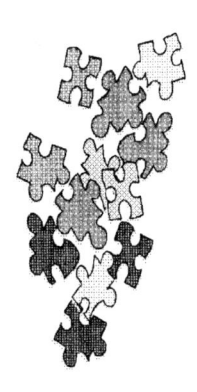

Jesse Underwood
My Great-Great-Grandfather

Jesse Underwood was born on July 13, 1804, in Bunscombe County, North Carolina to William and (?) Underwood. He came from a very large family. All of his brothers were Baptist preachers, including himself. He married Mary Elizabeth Ledbetter on December 25, 1822, in Haywood County, North Carolina. Mary was the daughter of Matthew and (?) Ledbetter. They remained in Haywood County and had eight children.
1. Francis Marion – September 28, 1824
2. Elijah Lidge – December 30, 1825
3. Margaret – April 6, 1827
4. William Riley – August 20, 1828
5. Gabriella Augustine – March 17, 1830
6. Daniel – October 11, 1831
7. Sarah E. August 23, 1833
8. John Asbury – June 12, 1835

Most of Jesse's brothers moved on about 1836. We aren't sure what caused this, but think it had to do with their stepmother. In 1836, Jesse and Mary moved their growing family to the rolling foothills of the Smokey Mountains in Roane County, Tennessee. There they had six more children.

9. Mary Catherine – December 4, 1836
10. Nancy Ann – April 6, 1838
11. Martha Jane – March 16, 1840
12. Walter K. – November 20, 1841
13. James Newton – April 23, 1843
14. Ruth Emiline – June 27, 1846

Written by Everett L. Hobbel
Reprinted here with permission

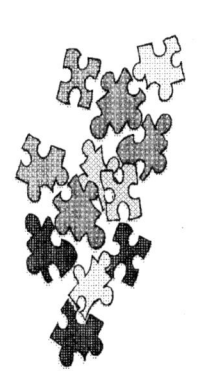

Reverend Jesse's Life and Family
Fifth Generation

The earliest documented information about our Underwood family comes from the family Bible of Jesse Underwood. This Bible, dated 1849 is very fragile and worn and is in the safekeeping of a great-granddaughter of Jesse's living in St. Louis, Missouri. This Bible states Jesse was born July 13, 1804. Census and other records state he was born in North Carolina.

Jesse married Mary Ledbetter on Christmas Day, 1822, according to his Bible. Mary was born July 23, 1802. Most records state Mary was born in North Carolina, but one record stated she was born in South Carolina.

Jesse and Mary (Ledbetter) Underwood are listed in the 1830 Federal Census of Haywood County, North Carolina with their first five children. Only age brackets are listed in the early Federal Census records. Their first eight children were born in Haywood County, North Carolina. They were: Francis Marion born 1824, Elijah born in 1825, Margaret born in 1827, William R. born in

1829, Gabriella born 1830, Daniel born 1831, Sarah E. born 1833, and John A. born 1835. Civil War records state that Francis, Daniel, and John were born in Haywood County, North Carolina.

Some time in 1836 Jesse and Mary removed to Roane County, Tennessee. All records indicate they lived there about twelve years and the remainder of their fourteen children were born there. They were: Mary C. born 1836, Nancy Ann born 1838, Martha Jane born 1840, Walter K. born 1841, James N. born 1843, and Ruth Emily born 1846.

On the fourth Saturday in July, 1844, four members of the Baptist clergy met in Roane County, Tennessee and founded the Cedar Fork Baptist Church. After this first meeting, seven original members were "Accepted by Letter" and Jesse, Polly (Mary) and their second son, Elijah, were three of these original members to join the church. On the fourth Saturday in August, 1844, Francis M., William R., and Gabriella A. Underwood joined the church. In December, 1844, Jesse was ordained to be a Baptist minister by this church and he received his "license to preach." Jesse served the church in several capacities for the next few years, including the pastor, or moderator as it was called back in those days. Three of the children got married while the family lived in Roane County, Tennessee. They were: Margaret married Sampson Mayfield in 1844, Elijah married Nancy Childers in 1845, and Gabriella married William K. Smith in 1847.

In 1847, Rev. Jesse Underwood and Mary with their large family removed to Union County, Illinois and settled near what is now Mt. Glenn. (Earlier it was believed they first settled on Bald Knob Mountain, but land records indicate they settled on Bald Knob some time about 1860 or later.) It seems very likely that right after the family arrived in Union County, Illinois, Rev. Jesse was instrumental in founding the Mt. Tabor Baptist Church that was located a few miles south of Alto Pass, Illinois and very close to Mt. Glenn. The earliest records from the American Baptist Historical Society in Rochester, New York state that Jesse was a delegate to the Baptist Association in 1848, and he was listed as Pastor of Mt. Tabor Baptist Church in 1850 and 1851. Jesse died September 26, 1851. Jesse's son, Elijah, is listed as a delegate to the Association in 1852. Elijah was killed in a railroad accident at Memphis, Tennessee in 1853. Mt. Tabor Church was torn down some time around 1900.

After Jesse died in 1851, Mary completed raising the large family, and she never married again. During the Civil War, five of the six living sons of Jesse and Mary fought in the conflict. Four brothers: Francis Marion, John Asbury, Daniel and James volunteered and fought for the Union Forces. One son, William R., went to Missouri and joined the Confederacy. The other son, Walter K., stayed home to run the farm and keep the family together. Walter used to haul water down to the Union Troops that were stationed nearby. In 1871 Walter lost his right hand by catching it in the machinery of a sawmill. Walter married Pheobe Caroline Nipper in 1863. Even though he was crippled, Walter was a successful farmer and his attention was given mostly to raising strawberries and raspberries.

Shortly after the Civil War, Francis Marion moved to what is now Clay County, Arkansas. He remained there the rest of his life and is buried in the Underwood Cemetery near Piggott, Arkansas. Some of Francis Marion's children were born in Illinois, but all of them grew up and lived in Arkansas. Some years later, about 1870, John Asbury removed to Clay County, Arkansas. All of his children grew up in this area and many of his descendants still live in the county. John became ill in 1883 and wanted to travel back to Union County, Alto Pass, Illinois to see his mother. He never recovered from the illness and died before he could return to Arkansas. He is buried at Mt. Tabor Cemetery in an unmarked grave. In 1899 Martha Jane (Underwood) Gore removed to Clay County, Arkansas. She lived there the rest of her life and is also buried in the Underwood Cemetery. Many of her descendants still live in the area. Some time shortly before 1900 another daughter of Jesse and Mary, Margaret (Underwood) Mayfield also removed to Arkansas where she lived the rest of her life and many of her descendants are still in the area.

Daniel Underwood died during the Civil War in Andersonville Prison, Georgia. His wife Susan (Pippins) Underwood continued to live in Union County, Illinois and raised their children. James N. Underwood came home from the Civil War in very poor health and died January 5, 1864 at his mother's home. Gabriella (Underwood) Smith, Sara (Underwood) Pippins, Nancy Ann (Underwood) Groves-Gore-Morgan, Walter K. Underwood and Ruth Emily (Underwood) Gore-Stone, stayed in Union County, Illinois and raised their families.

Many of their descendants still live in Southern Illinois. Mary C. (Underwood) Sams also stayed in Union County, Illinois, but very little is known about her or her supposed family. Sarah (Underwood) Pippins died young and is buried at Mt. Tabor Cemetery. She was supposed to have had a family, but as of now (1981), none of them have been located.

Mary (Ledbetter) Underwood died in 1894 at the age of 92 years. "She lived on her 80 acre farm near the top of Bald Knob Mountain near Alto Pass, Illinois for 45 years (?). By the time she was 80 years old, she had reared her children and helped with some of the grandchildren. She had saved some money and would quite often make loans to her neighbors to buy a cow or pay taxes, and she generally told them it had to be for that purpose or they didn't get any money," (as per W. E. Harris, a grandson). She always told her grandchildren, "It's not always what you make that counts, it's what you save." She is buried alongside of her husband, Jesse, at Mt. Tabor Cemetery, just South of Alto Pass, Illinois.

Additional Information

While in Tennessee, Jesse joined the Cedar Fork Baptist Church and was one of the first seven members on the fourth Sunday of July in 1844. He became an ordained minister on the last Sunday of December in 1844.

About 1847, Jesse and Mary moved their large family to Union County, Illinois. It is located near the bottom of Illinois, on the Mississippi River. The land was good, rich farmland, and the area was sparsely populated. The family had grown by now, Elijah, Margaret, and Gabriella all had married. They all farmed there, and Jesse started the Mt. Tabor Baptist Church. He was also selected as a delegate for the Baptist Ministry.

Jesse died August 9, 1851, in Union County, Illinois at the age of 47 years. He was buried in the Mt. Tabor Cemetery.

Mary still had several children at home at the time of Jesse's death. She raised them all to adulthood. During the war, she also helped to raise most of her grandchildren. She tended her 40-acre farm on Bald Knob, and taught her children the importance of saving money. She was able to lend her neighbors money for important things, as long as that's what the money went for.

Mary died January 3, 1894, in Union County, Illinois at the age of 92 years old. She is buried in the Mt. Tabor Cemetery beside Jesse.

> Written by Everett L. Hoebbel
> Reprinted here with permission

13/ MY LIFE IN BITS 'N' PIECES

Mary Elizabeth (Ledbetter) Underwood,
wife of Jesse Underwood
Born July 23, 1802
Married December 25, 1822, Haywood County, NC
Died January 3, 1894, Union County, Illinois

William Riley Underwood,
fourth child of Jesse and Mary Underwood
Born September 20, 1829, Haywood County, NC
Married January 6, 1850 to Nancy J. Green
Later married Sarah Mathis
Buried in the Underwood Cemetery Piggott, Arkansas

Daniel Underwood,
sixth child of Jesse and Mary Underwood
Born October 11, 1831, Haywood County, NC
Married March 6, 1853 to Susan A. Pippins
Died November 17, 1864, Andersonville, Georgia
as a P.O.W. during the Civil War

John Asberry Underwood,
eighth child of Jesse and Mary Underwood
Born June 12, 1835, Haywood County, NC
Married January 20, 1859 to Martha Smith
Married February 28, 1867 to Elizabeth Belew
Died August 17, 1883, Union County, Illinois

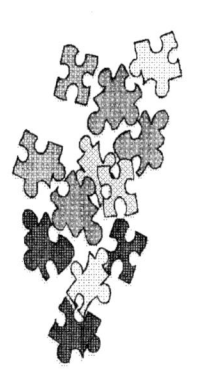

Francis Marion Underwood
My Great-Grandfather
Fourth Generation

Francis Marion Underwood was born in Haywood County, North Carolina, on September 28, 1824, to the Rev. Jesse and Mary (Ledbetter) Underwood. In 1836, he moved with his family to Roane County, Tennessee, and in 1847, the moved to Union County, Illinois. There was good, rich farmland there, and the area had few settlers.

After his family moved to Illinois, he met Susannah Vanncil of Union County. She had been born in Illinois about 1833, and her parents had both been born in Virginia. Francis and Susannah were married in Union County, on January 21, 1849.

They farmed and lived within a few miles of his parents' farm. They had six children:
1. Jesse—born November 1849, Union County, Illinois
2. Mary Eliza—born about 1853, Union County, Illinois
3. Ellen—born about 1855, Union County, Illinois
4. Francis Marion Jr.—born February 1858, Union County, Illinois
5. Jane—born about 1861, Union County, Illinois
6. John Henry—born April 1866, Union County, Illinois

Francis was one of five brothers that served in the Civil War. Four of the brothers served for the Union, from Illinois, and one went to Missouri to serve for the Confederacy. Francis enlisted on August 21, 1862, at Anna, in Union County, for three years and was mustered on September 11, 1862. He and his brothers were in Company "C" 109th Regiment, Illinois Infantry. Francis' rank was Musician Fifer (flute). At the time of his enlistment, he had light eyes, black hair and stood 5-foot, 9-inches. He and his brother, Daniel, deserted on December 20, 1862, at Holly Springs, Mississippi, during Grant's Central Mississippi Campaign. The Regiment was disbanded on April 10, 1863, having lost 237 men by desertion and Officers (except "K" Company) having proved themselves utterly incompetent. They were transferred to the 11th Illinois Infantry. He was returned to his Regiment on June 15, 1863, with loss of pay during his absence, Daniel was returned a short time later. He participated in the assaults on Vicksburg May 19 and 22, 1863, the surrender of Vicksburg on July 4, 1863, Action at Yazoo City, Mississippi on March 5, 1864, in which one of his brothers, John, was shot in the right hip, and Daniel was taken prisoner. Daniel died November 18, 1864, of malnutrition and diarrhea, 6½ months after he was captured at the famous Andersonville Prison Camp. He is buried at the site of the camp in grave #11091. Francis was also involved in the Siege of Spanish Fort and Fort Blakely in Alabama from March 26 through April 8, 1865, and the Assault and capture of Fort Blakely on April 9, 1865. He was discharged in Baton Rouge, Louisiana, on July 14, 1865. Francis received an Invalid Pension of twelve dollars a month from 1892 until his death, for the following conditions: loss of some eyesight, rheumatism, nervous condition, kidney disease, and catarrh of the head (chronic sinus condition).

Sometime between 1866 and 1869, he moved his family to Chalk Bluff Township, Green County, Arkansas. At that time, Green County covered most of Clay County, they were divided as they now are, before 1880. There, Francis was a blacksmith. Chalk Bluff is now a "vanished town" which was situated on Crowley's Ridge. It was the first trail into Northeastern Arkansas, from the Missouri Ozarks, because it was the only high land in a wilderness of swamps and backwater.

In the 1880 Federal Census, Francis had moved to nearby Haywood Township, Clay County, Arkansas. They probably moved about the time that Chalk Bluff fizzled out in the late 1870's. It was at that time that Francis took up farming again. In 1880, only Francis

Jr. and John Henry remained at home, and Jesse and his family lived next door to them with his family.

Susannah died before John Henry met Amanda Elizabeth Hodge, and they were married about 1889. Francis must have remarried, but I do not know the name of the woman. They had one son:

Jacob—born 1888

She must have died about 1892. On March 1893, he married Mrs. Amelia A. Pitts, age 40, of St. Francis. She died before the 1900 Census.

On or about January 16, 1902, Francis died at the age of 76 years, 3 months and 19 days. His cause of death, according to his attending physician, was "sickness." Jesse, Francis' oldest son, took over guardianship of Jacob, and a girl by the name of Luella Powers, who I believe might have been his stepdaughter or his granddaughter. There is no mention of Jacob after the 1900 Census, so I don't know what became of him.

Francis' estate was settled on October 2, 1902, with an estate sale. His three older sons bought items. One thing that caught my eye was the sale of a fife to John Henry. Could this possibly have been the one that Francis played while he was in the Civil War? We may never know for sure.

Written by Everett L. Hoebbel
Reprinted here with permission

21/MY LIFE IN BITS 'N' PIECES

Francis Marion Underwood Jr.,
Son of Francis Marion Sr. and Susannah
Born February 1858, Union County, Illinois
Arthur Underwood is standing in front of his father
Picture taken during the 1890's

John Henry—My Grandfather
Third Generation

John Henry Underwood was born April 1866, in Union County, Illinois to Francis Marion and Susannah Vancil Underwood. He was born after his father had been home from the Civil War for about a year. Not long after his birth, his parents moved the family to Green County, Arkansas, which was later changed to Clay County, Arkansas.

John was a tall man, he stood about 6-foot, 1-inch. He was a kind-hearted man, I have been told, and very strong. He could lift an anvil with one hand. He did many various jobs. He was a carpenter, a blacksmith, a farmer, a music teacher, and a Magistrate.

He met Amanda Elizabeth Hodge while giving her music lessons. She was the daughter of Moses and Hulda Hodge. They fell in love and were married about 1888. There is no record of this, because the Courthouse burned down in 1893, and all of the records were destroyed. They had ten children:

1. Beulah—born December 1890
2. Homer Byron—born August 7, 1894
3. Bernie Bethel—born October 2, 1895

4. Bertha—born June 1897
5. and 6. Chester and Lester—born 1899 (died within a day of birth)
7. Maude—born April 3, 1901
8. Marshal Neil—born 1903 (died 1905)
9. Hubert Hackson—born February 20, 1905
10. John—born 1907 (died a few months after birth)

John and Amanda were Baptist, and John was also a preacher, though he didn't practice it. At his fathers' estate sale in 1902, John bought a feather bed for $6.50, a rocking chair for $.50, and the fife that his father played in the Civil War for $.25. One of his children in later years lost it. He taught each of his children music to some degree. He thought that was a talent the family should have.

John was working on a frosty barn roof in February 1907, when he slid and fell off of it. He broke ribs, which punctured his lungs and caused gangrene. He died a week later on February 7, 1907, and is buried in the Underwood Cemetery.

Amanda was either pregnant with John or had just had him. He died not long after birth also. Amanda supported her family by taking in laundry, tatting, embroidery, sewing, quilting and working in the fields. About four months after John's death, while Amanda was in the fields with the children, the house that she and John had shared burned to the ground.

I think it was about this time that Amanda moved her family to Dunklin County, Missouri. Her family had moved there a few years earlier. I was not able to find them listed on the 1910 Federal Census, because the records were in such poor condition. I did find

25/MY LIFE IN BITS 'N' PIECES

Homer living with her elderly parents, probably helping to take care of the farm.

Amanda loved to read, especially mysteries and Zane Grey westerns. She helped to raise several of her grandchildren. She was a wonderful cook, she loved music, and to dance. She had beautiful flower gardens, and was proud of her Irish heritage.

Amanda died September 8, 1968, in the Dunklin County Hospital, Kennett, Missouri of cancer. She is buried in the Cardwell Cemetery, Cardwell, Missouri.

Written by Kim Kester
1321 North 31st Street
Sheboygan, WI 53031
Reprinted here with permission

More About John Henry Underwood

John Henry Underwood was born in April of 1866 in Union County, Illinois. He met Amanda E. Hodge while he was her music teacher. They fell in love and were married about 1889. Amanda was born in Arkansas to Moses and Hulda Hodge on April 25, 1871. Aside from being a music teacher, John was also a carpenter. In the year 1900 he was a Magistrate. Amanda was Irish through and through, even had the red hair. They had ten children, six of whom lived to adulthood.

1. Beulah was born December 1890. She married Johnny Stewart, and they had two children. Golden was born about 1908, and Kitty was born about 1910. Then Beulah married a second husband, Millard Williams. They had two children also. Carmen was born about 1914, and Louis was born about 1916. I'm not sure just when Beulah died.
2. Homer Byron was born August 1892. He married Cassie Hamilton. They had six children: Juanita was born 1918, Cleatus was born 1920, Mavis L. was born 1922, Oren was born 1924, Jewell was born 1926, and Carl Buell was born 1928. Cassie died 1930. Homer remarried, Macie L. Jackson, in 1931. To them were born five children: Jerry Wayne was born 1932, Homer Jr. was born 1935, Winfred was born 1937, Caroline was born 1939, and Joyce was born 1941. Homer Sr. died in 1944 of cancer.
3. Bernie Bethel was born October 2, 1895, in Piggott, Clay County, Arkansas. He married Ruth Alice Nixon on December 23, 1916, in Kennett, Dunklin County, Missouri. They had six children, five of whom lived to adulthood: Bonita Laverne was born April 26, 1919; Fay (Gene) was born July 28, 1921; Billy Burke was born August 10, 1924; Bryce Berniel was born October 17, 1930, and died July 7, 1931; Jon Stanley was born October 12, 1933; and Alice Elizabeth was born July 15, 1937. Bernie died May 24, 1970. Ruth died July 29, 1973.

4. Bertha was born June 1897. She married Otho Hartsoe. They had: twin boys, Max and Vernon were born 1920; Peggy Jean was born 1922; and Caroline was born 1936. Bertha died 1973 of cancer.
5. Maude was born April 3, 1901. She married Joe Williams. They had: twins, Wanda and Marilyn, were born 1920; and Theda Bara was born 1922.
6. Marshall Neil, born about 1903, was named for a beautiful yellow rose. He died 1903 or 1904 as an infant.
7. Hubert Jackson (Jack) was born 1904. He married Mary Nixon Lemon. They had four children: Glendon was born October 18, 1933; Patsy Ruth was born in 1935; Norman Joe was born July 30, 1937; and Susie was born July 14, 1942.

At Francis Marion Underwood's estate sale, John bought a feather bed, a rocking chair and a fife. The fife was believed to be the one Francis Marion used while in the Civil War.

John H. fell from a frosty barn roof one morning while at work. He lingered for eight days and then died. He was buried in the Piggott Cemetery with four of his infant children, John, Marshall and a set of twins. This was about 1903 or 1904.

Amanda moved her family to Dunklin County, Missouri in 1909. She supported her family any way she could, cooking, sewing or whatever. She died September 8, 1968, in the Dunklin County Hospital, Kennett, Missouri. She is buried in the Cardwell Cemetery in Cardwell, Missouri.

John Henry Underwood,
Son of Francis Marion & Susannah Vancil Underwood
Born April 1866, Union County, Illinois
Died 1907, Clay County Arkansas

29/MY LIFE IN BITS 'N' PIECES

Amanada Elizabeth (Hodge) Underwood,
Daughter of Moses and Hulda Delila (Gibbs) Hodge
Born April 25, 1871, in Arkansas
Married John Henry Underwood in 1889
Died September 8, 1968, Kennett, Missouri
She is buried in the Cardwell Cemetary in Cardwell,
Missouri

Moses Hodge,
Father of Amanda Elizabeth (Hodge) Underwood

31/MY LIFE IN BITS 'N' PIECES

Hulda Delila (Gibbs) Hodge,
Mother of Amanda Elizabeth (Hodge) Underwood
Born February 11, 1824
Her mother was Nancy T. Gibbs, who was born in
1796

Bernie Bethel Underwood—My Father

Bernie Bethel Underwood was born October 2, 1895, in Piggott, Clay County, Arkansas. His father died while he was a child. He quit school to work in a sawmill to help his mother support the family. In later years, shortly before WWI started, he lost his left index finger in a stave mill, so he was unable to serve his country. He married Ruth Alice Nixon on December 23, 1916, in Kennett, Dunklin County, Missouri. They had six children of which five reached adulthood. Below are their names:

Bonita Laverne, born on April 26, 1919, married Otis Harman in 1936. They had seven children: Darrell was born June 20, 1938; Edna June was born June 29, 1940; Sherman Jack was born July 8, 1942; Billy Gene was born February 28, 1944; Paul David was born June 1, 1946; Donna was born October 17, 1950; and Joe Wayne was born in 1954. Bonita later married Horrace Johnston. They had one child who died a few months after birth.

Fay Imogene was born July 28, 1921. She married James Davis, who turned out to be a bigamist. No divorce was needed. She married Roy Francis Key

August 12, 1946. They had seven children: Roy Jr. was born May 16, 1947; Regina Gail was born July 2, 1949; Billy Jon was born October 25, 1953; Starlyn Carol was born September 16, 1955; Lee Ann Holly was born May 22, 1957; Melodi Rae was born September 30, 1960; and Quaita Jahree was born January 21, 1964. Gene met Dennis Snyder in 1970. They married and divorced in 1975.

Billy Burke was born on August 10, 1924. He married Lucille Hollis in September 1946. They had five children: Nikki Carol was born October 13, 1947; Linda Kay was born October 26, 1949; Phillip Anthony was born December 30, 1951; Eddie was born February 17, 1959; and Michael was born February 22, 1962. Billy later married Betty Jean Young. They had one son, Christopher Cole He was born January 3, 1979, and died on October 12, 1979. Billy died April 7, 1988, from cancer.

Bryce Berniel was born October 17, 1930. He died July 7, 1931.

Jon Stanley was born October 12, 1933. He married Mary Anne Edwards in 1950. They had five children: Joe Wayne was born in 1956; David was born in 1958; Mark was born in 1960; Suzann was born in 1963; and Scotty.

Alice Elizabeth was born July 15, 1937. She married James Kester June 8, 1953. They had two sons. Donald Gene was born March 9, 1954. Dana Andrew was born January 25, 1955. She had Allan with Gerald LaFerney. Allan took the name of Kester. Alice later married Albert Cisco. They had three children: Terry L. was born April 25, 1962, and died a few hours later; Marti Lari was born March 9, 1965; and Lisa Jeanette was born August 21, 1966.

35/MY LIFE IN BITS 'N' PIECES

Bernie was a carpenter by trade and built many homes in his lifetime, some in Van Buren County, Michigan. He loved to hunt when he was young. There was a joke that he painted all of his cars John Deere green. He died of cancer on May 24, 1970.

Ruth loved reading and loved flowers. She was a stern parent and grandparent, but loved all her grandchildren dearly. She died July 29, 1973, in the Jonesboro Hospital in Jonesboro, Arkansas.

Bernie and Ruth are buried in the Farmhill Cemetery at Harrisburg, Arkansas.

Bernie Bethel Underwood (center)
Born October 2, 1895
With friends Elmer and Joe Williams
This picture was taken about 1915 when Bernie was 20 years old.

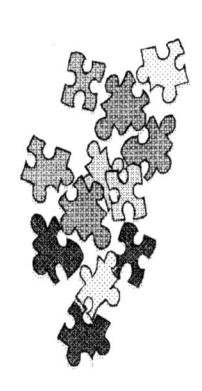

Fay Imogene (Gene) Underwood Key

I was born on July 28, 1921, in Dunklin County, Missouri. I grew up in and around the Missouri-Arkansas line. I married James Davis on February 10, 1940. I found out later he was married and had a family in his home state of Texas. That was not acceptable to me, so the marriage was off. Then on August 12, 1946, I married Roy Francis Key in Manila, Arkansas. We had seven children:
1. Roy Francis Key, Jr. was born May 16, 1947. He married Katheryn Johnson January 1969. They only had one girl, Terry Lynn Key. Terry married Daniel Abbot. They have Nicholas Abbot.
2. Regina Gail was born July 2, 1949. She married Waymon Raper, and they have two children. Kellie Marie was born November 29, 1978, and Shannon Wayne was born August 18, 1982. Kellie has two sons, Damian and Cameron.
3. Billy Jon was born October 25, 1953. He married Sherree Provost in 1977. They have two children. Keri Jon was born July 5, 1977, and Teah Marie was born January 17, 1981.

4. Starlyn Carol was born September 16, 1955. She married John Wesley Stoup October 1989. They have no children.
5. Lee Ann Holly was born May 22, 1957. She married Darrell Dean Graves December 8, 1983. Joey Dean was born April 28, 1979. Michelle Lee Ann was born December 8, 1983.
6. Melodi Rae was born September 30, 1960. She has two sons by Dale VerHey. They carry their father's name. Michael Dale was born October 29, 1983, and Chad Allen was born July 29, 1986.
7. Quaita Jahree was born on January 21, 1964. She married Paul Bridges. Ashley Ann was born August 13, 1984, and Joshua Paul was born November 1, 1987.

I have two other grandchildren, Dale and Raeann, that I love very much. But I don't know too much about them, as I've never been around them. They don't have our name.

Where I Came From

I've had a feeling for days that I'd like to write something about my Grandma Underwood. She is the only one of my grandparents that I ever knew, and so maybe that's the reason she seems so special. Or maybe she was real special. She never did anything spectacular, that I know of, but she was a person you could not forget.

I am told, through an extensive family tree, that she and my grandfather also came to Arkansas from Southern Illinois. I have no idea how they got there. But I'm also told that my grandfather's folks traveled by wagon and horses from North Carolina through Tennessee, then to Illinois, and from there to Arkansas.

My grandfather was a carpenter. He died from a fall from a barn roof that he was building. The records say he was thirty-six years old at the time. My grandmother was left with six children and another one yet unborn at her husband's death. She had already buried three infants, a set of twins and another one. The fourth baby died soon after her husband died. I believe her life was very hard.

I don't know how she provided for her family. She may have had to live in a house with others and help with the sewing, cooking, cleaning, and other chores, and even going to the field to work. Most women of that day went to the cotton fields. This continues even today. But since there are machines to do most of the hardest work, it is quite different from my gramma's day. I know she hired out as a cook at the lumber and sawmill camps to be able to feed her children. Some of the older ones were soon out on their own, married or otherwise.

My grandmother was in no danger of rape or abuse or harassment, for those words had not been used, or even written at the time. She was held in high esteem by all who knew her. She became a midwife and quite a good doctor over the years. It all came through experience. People from all around sent for her when their wives were due to deliver or when their children got sick. It was an everyday thing for my mother to say to Dad, "Bernie, you'd better go get your mom. This kid is really sick." A way of life!

Sometimes Gramma lived with us. I don't recall the reason, she just did. And we kids loved it! No, she didn't play dolls or marbles with us. She was kept on a high pedestal. She was Gramma. No other reason was needed. We loved her. We respected her. We held her in a sort of awe!

I remember her long, thick braid of hair that she let hang down when she wasn't going out. We loved to touch her hair. My younger brother called it "Gramma's long down."

She lived to be 97 years old. She ate whatever was before her and never ever heard of cholesterol, enzymes, or pollution. She had a theory about food:

"Eat what's before you, and thank God for it." A pretty good idea, don't you think? I know it has worked for me and mine.

I am 72 years old, and I work one day a week caring for a lady who is 97 years old. I'm struck speechless with the difference in her life and that of my gramma.

This lady is a national treasure, at least, that's what I tell her. She has three well-to-do children who live in New York, Arizona and California. I guess they visit her, but I've not seen any of them since I've worked for her. But I'm told someone will be here at the Christmas holiday.

This lady lives in and owns a nice brick condo, has lovely furniture in it, has the best and most nutritious food that can be bought, and sits here with caregivers who are all strangers to her. There are six of us who stay with her around the clock. We love her and take the best care of her, but we are strangers.

My gramma lived in houses full of relatives, did her part of the work (as long as she could), shared her life with her family, and died with many loved ones around her bed. Her name is revered still. "What do you think Gramma would do?" is a common question in our family. What more could a person ask for? She gave love. She received love. I'd say she lived a good life. A full life!

My Father, the Storyteller

My father told us many stories as we sat around the wood-burning heater after supper at night. There were no radios to entertain us, nor were there TVs to baby-sit us. So we had to "make do" with what we had. But it was fun, and we really loved what we did have—family.

My father had a lovely musical voice. He almost always had a duet, trio, or a quartet of singers that sang together. I loved it when he sang bass, and I loved it when he sang tenor. I guess I loved just about everything he did. He was very easy to love.

I remember so many stories he used to tell us. We usually sat in the dark, around the heater, for no one liked the kerosene lamps we had to use. And we loved the stories he told us. Here are a couple.

There was a gang of young men going to the Saturday night dance out in the bayou country. They had to travel several miles in boats to get across this body of water. Three men in a boat was about par for the course. But when the boat seemed to be too low in the water, my dad had to ask one guy to climb out and into a tree to wait until he could take some of his load to the dance and return for the other guy, who just happened to be his cousin, Willie Hodge. So Willie climbed the tree, and Dad and Jim continued on to the dance with full intentions of going back for his cuz. But upon arriving at the party, where it was nice and warm, the brightness of the lights from lanterns was very enticing. Combine this with friends, food, drinks and much more fun to be had, well, they sort of forgot about Willie. In fact, he was the last thought on anyone's mind. So he sat in the tree until the party was over, and the folk started home.

As you probably know, an oar boat don't leave ruts in the water, so it was quite by accident that someone got close enough to the tree to hear him calling out for a ride.

My dad always got a chuckle out of that story. My Uncle Willie saw it in an altogether different light!

And now for the second story. It also has to do with a group of young guys going to a Saturday night dance. And it is about the shock of a lifetime as they went home. But I think I'll let my son relate the story the way he remembers it.

This son is now 46 years old, and he wrote the story for one of his classes in the seventh grade in 1960. I have his original copy, which my mother had kept all the years since Roy Jr. wrote it. When she died, someone saw it and asked me if I wanted it. And, of course, I did. I still have the original little scribbled story. I'm including it in this chapter of my life. So now it has become a part of my records that I hope to pass down to my kids. Just one more of my treasures!

After Roy wrote this in his English class, it was printed in the South Haven Tribune.

45/MY LIFE IN BITS 'N' PIECES

Roy Key
7th/hr.
Nov. 2, 1961
English

My Grandfather is about six 2. He is 164 years old. His hair is gray and he stands straight not stooped.
One time when he was a young man before he got married he was acting smart. Him and his boyfriend and two girls were walking through the woods going home. Up ahead my grandfather saw a stump. He thought he'd jump it and show the girls what a good jumper he was. He ran up and jump it just as he got halfway across it turned out to be a big black bull. The bull let out a roar and took off with my grandfather on his back. About an hour later my grandfather came in all scratch up. That was the last time he jumped a stump at night.

This is a picture of the Roy Key early family taken in 1948. The little boy is the storywriter of the above article.

The Greatest Guy I Ever Knew

I awakened this morning with a great desire to write something down on paper that would serve as a tribute to a man I once knew and loved dearly. I am 74 years old, and my mind is very good yet. It is one of the blessings in life that I am most grateful for. A good mind is to be cherished, I feel! II Timothy 1:7 says, "For God hath not given us the spirit of fear; but of power, and of love, and of a sound mind." And I'm very grateful. I claim a sound mind as a gift from God. I entertain NO thoughts of Alzheimer's disease.

One of my earliest memories is of my brother. He was less than a year old, so I was less than four. I can't describe the particulars, but I was playing with him by the window. I was making him cry, so I could love and pet and coddle him to get him to stop crying. It sounds mean, but it wasn't. I wasn't hurting him, but I knew how to make him cry. And I did that so I'd have the excuse to just love him to pieces. It always seemed to work.

He was always so very special to me! This little incident happened in the spring of 1925. I was not four until July of 1925.

Then another thing I remember was in 1928. This time I did hurt my brother, but it was an accident. My older sister and I were having some kind of confrontation. We didn't actually fight much. Our folks wouldn't tolerate fighting each other, only FOR each other. That was allowed! I don't recall the details of this incident. I only remember the feeling of being trapped.

My sister had gotten the little brother on her side. I might've been a little jealous. I do recall picking up the first thing I could grab, and it was a one-gallon kerosene can, pouring spout and all. I began to turn round and round.

My sister talked the little brother into charging in. I'm not sure what he was supposed to do when he got in the center of this action. But he was four and he charged. And I couldn't stop whirling, so the spout hit his head. He screamed. I screamed. Our sister screamed. The blood squirted from his scalp injury.

It was a trauma I've never forgotten. My sister ran to get Mama, and we had another trauma to endure. Needless to say, we all lived over it.

This is a picture of my brother, Billy Burke Underwood, my best friend, when he was six years old.

His face wasn't dirty. He'd fallen off his tricycle and was pinned against the heater. It looked worse at the time it happened than it did in this picture. Wow! Look at them bib overalls! A 1930 special!

49/MY LIFE IN BITS 'N' PIECES

Next, I remember some very good times he and I had in 1932 and 1933. He had gotten a Coaster wagon for Christmas. We learned how to entertain ourselves for days and days with this wagon. Being children from the farm, we knew how to hitch each other up to pull the wagon while the other one rode. We changed up from time to time. I don't remember ever quarreling about whose time it was to ride and whose time it was to pull.

The first time around the house went pretty slow. But as time and experience took over, the puller went faster and faster, and the driver stood up in the wagon and lashed the "horse" with a seagrass rope. We screamed our way around that house until we were both worn out. We made deep ruts, just like the old pioneers.

I went back in 1991 and made a picture of the house in which we lived in 1932 and 1933. A lot of things have changed since then!

Time went on, we moved on, and in about two years, I had the misfortune of discovering BOYS. Boys that were not my brothers. My brother and I didn't grow apart, we just had different interests. Suddenly, I didn't like shooting marbles, playing leap-frog, and things like that.

A little aside here. I was no longer trying to cram myself into those little bitsy overalls of my brothers. You know, in the 20's and 30's, and even the 40's, girls didn't wear "men's clothing." But I did get into these tiny little overalls a few times before I grew up. They were so small they almost did permanent damage to my anatomy. But I survived that too!

I got married in 1940. BIG MISTAKE! My brother went into the Navy in 1942. This is a picture of him in the South Pacific. He's the one in the middle of the back row.

He was 19 years old then. I still have every letter he wrote me from all those "exotic-sounding" islands. But, of course, the islands weren't exotic, at all. They were mostly full of dead, young men. I have all of my brother's battle stars, good conduct ribbons, and the like. Why would I get them, you may ask? I guess it was that unseen bond we always had between us. It was always there. He was the greatest guy. (Note: this picture and a two-page letter about Billy Underwood's experiences during WWII are included on pages 158 and 159 of Tom Brokaw's third book, *An Album of Memories* published by Random House in NYC, 2001.)

Then in 1946, he came home from the war. He and I both got married that year. His first time, my second. We had our first children within five months of each other. Two years later, we had our second children three months apart. We kept close all of our lives.

In 1951 my husband and I came to Michigan. About two or three years later my brother and his family came to Michigan also. He died here in 1988 and is buried here. I'm still here too, but not buried yet!

I don't believe I have ever been mad at him. I disapproved of his divorce, in later years, but was not mad. I always felt there was some kind of reason for anything he did. (I never did find the reason for his divorce.) But we were still close. I even ran around with him and his second wife. Not because of any love or respect for her, but I was determined nothing would come between my brother and me. And it never did!

This is a picture of Billy when he first came to live in Michigan. He was 34 years old at the time.

He lived to be 63 years old before he succumbed to cancer. We saw a lot of good times and a lot of bad times in our lives, but we were always close. We never lost that brother/sister bond we shared. Together, my brother and I saw our parents through life, and also their deaths. We made many trips from our homes to Arkansas where our parents lived. He always paid most of the expenses for the trips—He paid his way and most of mine. He was generous beyond belief. He always took care of his family's needs, even after he developed quite a drinking problem.

And then, in 1987, he was told he had cancer with four to six months to live. I think I could have stood it better had it been me instead of him. And then we became closer still. I went to his home everyday, with few exceptions, and we talked. We discussed sixty years of our lives together. I wish I'd kept a tape recorder with me, so I could have recorded all the conversations. But I didn't. Now it's too late. But I have them all in my memory.

His death hurt me more than anything I've ever had to face. It's been nearly seven years now, and it still hurts. But I've learned to live with it. It does get easier with time.

Here's one last picture of him and me. He was 61, and I was 64.

53/MY LIFE IN BITS 'N' PIECES

Billy was a good man. Everybody ought to have a brother like mine!

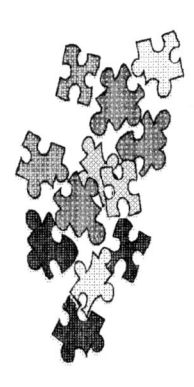

My Connection to Richard Nixon

My mother, Ruth Alice (Nixon) Underwood, was very proud of her name! My mother was born on November 26, 1897, to David and Alice Arthor Nixon near Kennett, Missouri. Alice was David's second wife and a niece to his first wife, who had been dead for some time.

He had five children by his first wife and then had six more by the second wife. My mother was #4 in the second family of children. I know very little about the first five people, but as I am not doing a family tree, I guess it doesn't matter that much.

After my grandparents had their sixth child, my grandmother developed tuberculosis. This lady died in about 1905, and it is about this sad event that I am writing. As you may or may not know, there weren't any drugs or sanitariums for T.B. patients in the early 1900's. The doctors told their patients to go to the mountains where the air was purer and live as long as they could. That was their only hope. So when my grandfather saw no other way out, he undertook a trip by wagon. He took his four small children and headed for the Ozark Mountains, seeking a cure for his sick wife. It doesn't seem very far now, but look at a map and try to imagine starting a trip of that magnitude in a covered wagon with all of those small kids and a very sick wife. He was heading for Boonville, Arkansas, which now has a large, modern facility for the treatment of tuberculosis.

I have no way of knowing how long these people were on the road, but I do know that my grandmother died before they got to Boonville. They were somewhere near Harrison, Arkansas when she died. And she's buried where she died. We've not been able to determine exactly where, though we've tried. Courthouses have burned down and there were no computers to store important documents in. We'll probably never know the exact spot.

So, be that as it may, "the trip" was what caught my attention. I was very intrigued with this part of the story, and I've never forgotten what I was told.

My mother was eight years old at the time, and this story was passed down from a child's memory to another child—me. So this is as near the truth as I am able to ascertain.

After the funeral, my grandfather gathered his children and began the long journey back to his farm in southeastern Missouri. Now this was before Ramada and Holiday Inns had taken root and started to grow. So this miniature wagon train stopped along the way to cook food on a campfire by the roadside. On one such evening, as a meal of fried potatoes and whatever else was being cooked, to everyone's surprise three dark shadowy figures slipped noiselessly out of the deeper shade of the forest and crept up to the light of the campfire.

My grandfather was probably startled, and the children were terrified. But the Indians (yes, absolutely wild Indians) were not collecting scalps. They were hungry! This was ascertained by their gestures and such. So Grandfather fed them and continued on his way home.

After this, the Indians followed the small party (at a discreet distance, of course) and showed up each evening and insisted on having dinner with their newfound friends. Eventually, Grandfather got tired of cooking for uninvited guests, or he was running out of potatoes. I don't know which, but he decided it was time to draw the line. He said enough is enough. He was tired of feeding or sharing his kids' food with outsiders. So when the three guys slid in for their handout, Grandfather told them to get lost, or something like that.

The men, not being well versed in the English language, kept coming in closer with their hands out, begging. Grandfather kept saying no, and he kept the lid on the fried potatoes. Eventually the spuds needed stirring. So when the lid came up and Granddad tried to stir his food with his favorite knife, one man reached in the skillet and grabbed a handful of potatoes. Without planning or thinking, Granddad gave the man's hand a whack with his butcher knife and cut it quite seriously. The three stooges left promptly. They didn't come back. Mission accomplished, I guess.

My granddad returned home, in time, with the children. I don't know how long all of this took. Granddad tried to pick up his life and go on, but found he could not farm his land, do all the things he needed to do, and give his children, especially three small girls, the care and attention they needed. So, one of his daughters who was married, volunteered to keep the small girls a while and help her dad raise them.

After about a year, the girls returned home to their father. At that time my mother was nine or ten years old. She began doing the cooking, housekeeping, and caring for two younger sisters. She did the family laundry and got the three of them off to school. And this was in the era of zinc washtubs and scrub-boards. Sound impossible? I have a theory about things that seem impossible. I think when you are given a tough job to do, you will be given the courage and strength to do the job, no matter what it is.

So that was my mother's lot in life at a very young age, and she did her best. She proved equal to the task. But I'd hate to see the "wimps" of the 90's put in a similar situation. I can just hear it now. "What is that goofy-looking thing, and what am I supposed to do with it? Is that a new model Nintendo game?"

I can hear my mother say, "My Dear, that's the way we do our laundry. And after you hang them on the line to dry, you can bring them in and iron them."

And now for the rest of the Nixon connection. In 1962, Richard Nixon began to get a lot of publicity because he was running for president. My mother and her two sisters got real excited about this, because they shared his last name.

It was announced he was going to be at a fundraiser in Flint, Michigan on a certain day. My Aunt Emily, who had lived in Flint since 1929, began writing and calling his office trying to get an appointment with him, knowing it would be next to impossible with his busy schedule. She only wanted to be able to ask him a couple of questions about his family to find out if there really was a connection between their families. Aunt Emily stayed by her phone and watched the mail with all diligence, but in vain.

When the day of the fund-raiser came, my aunt was terribly disappointed and ready to admit defeat. Then, to her great surprise, the phone rang. It was his personal secretary asking, could she come down to the banquet hall and meet him? And, of course, she could. So she rushed down to the hall, puffing and panting, walked into the room, looked around for him, and finally saw and made eye contact with him.

He rushed over, tweaked her nose and said, "Anyone can tell that's a Nixon nose." Needless to say, he made her day! She explained why she had wanted to speak to him. He told her some information on his side of the family. He said he was much too busy to follow up on it, but wished her luck in her search for a family connection.

My Aunt Emily is now deceased. So is my mother. So is my Aunt Mary. So the three little Nixon girls of the long ago wagon train trip are all dead. There's no one left who knows anything, or cares. So I guess we'll never know for sure. We never did get any concrete evidence that we were related. No actual records. We only have what he told my Aunt Emily, by mouth. His father was my grandfather's cousin. So whatever that makes him in my life, I guess I'll take it. I can't brag, can I? Maybe I don't really want to. I guess it depends on where you stand when you look at the situation.

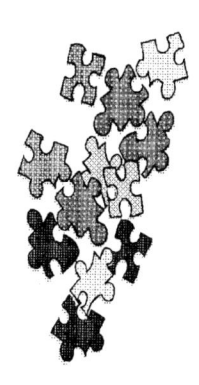

Some Things I Remembered

For many years—actually, most of my adult life—I've wanted to write. Not that all of my life has been unusually bad or good. I just wanted to write! But now that I've talked myself into it, I'm not at all sure how to start, or what I'm going to say. That's why I call it, My Life in Bits 'N' Pieces. This is probably the beginning of my life's story. I may include bits of prose or poetry. It may be more like a diary or a journal, but not a day by day entry. Maybe more like a year by year account of my life. But I must write, and I feel better now that I've begun. I think it will be easier if I break it down into years.

This all began a very long time ago. I was born to a father that was so honest it was unreal by today's standards, and a mother of equal integrity. She had a religious background. And I've found out recently that he did too, although I never thought of him in that way. To us, he was all the god we needed.

My father was a carpenter and a farmer, who never made much money at either of his occupations. Yet, we never thought of ourselves as being poor or deprived. I'll bet my mother did! We children who were born before, and grew up during, and having survived to tell the story of The Great Depression, never felt poor. Everybody was poor, and we fit in nicely. Now, when I see my children waste so much on their children, I look back and know I was poor. And I'm appalled at the waste! I do believe it is sinful. It ought to be against the law! When I express this to my children, they come back with, "But Mom, this is the 90's." And I guess that's supposed to make me feel better—make it okay.

Now to put this in perspective, I have to say, we lived in Arkansas for the first thirty years of my life. I was fortunate in having grown up before the word "babysitter" had been coined. Come to think of it, a lot of things had not been invented, like cars, TVs, electric iron, razors, washers and dryers, refrigerators, radio and Nintendos. Now tell me, how did I survive without a Nintendo?

Remember the faithful outhouse? Anybody? This was before that dude was moved inside under the same roof with all our other goodies. And we were a happy family. My dad made the living. He came home every night. Our mom kept the house, cooked the food, made a garden and canned lots of food for the winter, and quilted quilts. She sewed some of our clothes on an old treddle-powered Singer sewing machine. She made some of our underthings from flour sacks. We were right in style. Everybody else did too.

There was a movie on TV recently called, Fried Green Tomatoes. Now please don't laugh. That's good food! If you like it, I mean, and I do. I remember taking fried okra to school in a homemade biscuit for my lunch. And let me tell you something, it was good. And fried potatoes weren't bad either. You might be surprised how little it took to make us happy. No one had heard of Eskimo Pies, ice cream on a stick, Oreo cookies, or Pepsi. I guess we were luckier than we knew then.

Now in 2000, as I rewrite all of this stuff, I see that I have often repeated myself. You see, I wrote down remembrances as they came to me. And I apologize here for repeating segments. I'm sure I have.

So to go back to the beginning. Having been born in 1921, I have to admit I don't remember much about 1922 or 1923. But I do remember an earth-shaking moment in 1924. My parents, one sister, and I were at church. My mom was expecting my first brother. I remember my mom taking me outside to relieve myself. I was only three, and my mom carried me outside. When she sat me down behind a bush and away from the lights that were streaming out from the open door, she accidentally put my foot directly on a pinching bug.

Do you know what a pinching bug is? I thought not, so I'll tell you! He can get to be an inch and a half long. He has a hard, brown shell-like covering. He has two little horn-like thingies coming out of the sides of his head. Their intended use is to suck the blood out of other living things for food. But when you step on him in a dark churchyard, and you're barefooted, he will grab your toe and hang on for dear life!

And he did. And all the screaming and jumping in the world won't persuade him to let go until you land on him, and he probably gets knocked unconscious and has to let go.

Thus I was introduced to the dark and seamy side of life. I decided early in life, things weren't going to be easy. A month later, my brother was born, and things took a turn for the better. I had no idea at that time how very much I would love him all the days of his life. He died of cancer in 1988 at the age of 63, and I truly felt that a part of me had died also. I still can't think of it without pain, and it's been over six years.

The year 1925 is a complete blank. But I do remember 1926 and 1927, because we lived in the same house both years. And I vividly remember the big flood of 1927. Down south every spring there is a flood, but some floods are more devastating than others. 1927 was a bad one. Let me explain. We lived in the Mississippi River Delta where the land is as level as a dining room table, no hills and valleys and that sort of thing. Our house sat just a tiny bit higher than most other houses, for our yard was not entirely covered with water. So all the neighbors brought their cows, mules, horses, chickens, and even pigs and turned them loose on our little island in all the water.

Even though I was less than six years old, I remembered poor Noah and all of his trials, and I could duly sympathize with him. My dad built a boat, not an ark, to get us to wherever we had to go. Like, to the barn to feed the animals, or to the chicken house to gather eggs. And we also went across the gravel road to help take care of an elderly couple. And soon the flood of 1927 was history.

Then came 1928. I remember where we lived, for I started to school that year. It wasn't called kindergarten then, but primer. I know we sat in red chairs around a long brown table. And because I was too shy to ask to go to the outhouse, I wet my clothes. The red chair left a lasting impression on the backside of my dress, and then total humiliation set in like a case of gangrene. Therefore I remember a part of 1928.

Then in 1929, the banks busted. At least, that's what Dad told us. He just came home from town, and everybody was excited or agitated or something. I didn't know what was going on, but I knew something was different. As for the banks' problems, that didn't interest us. We didn't have anything in them. We didn't see any outward change in our lives. Our cow still had to be milked twice a day. The chickens still laid eggs, the garden had to be planted, as did the cotton, corn and soybeans. Later, it all had to be harvested. And so goes 1929. Nothing out of the ordinary, or so we thought at the time. We didn't realize what an earth-shaking event was happening. Nor did we realize that the entire United States of America would be feeling the results of it for many years to come. In fact, things are still compared to and measured by "The Great Depression." Twas a bad time for all.

Then came 1930 and 1931. We again, lived in the same house for two years. Not too often did this happen. We usually moved every year. My father was better known as a sharecropper, rather than a carpenter, although he still had all his skills as a carpenter. So we moved often. We had different houses and landlords, but the crops we planted and harvested were the same. People can't live without cotton products. And the animals can't live without corn or soybeans. So there it is. All settled!

In 1930 my second brother was born. He died in 1931, less than a year old. We have absolutely nothing to show for his life, not even a picture! Only our memories. And I do remember the terrible wails of my mother and the way my dad walked around like a horse had kicked him in the stomach. I was about ten at the time, and it didn't effect me then as much as it does now. I still have times of grief for the little boy that never had the chance to grow up and experience life as we know it. I believe it's all right to grieve, if it's not overdone. It's healthy to grieve some. Grief helps bring healing to the heart and spirit. And so goes 1931.

But besides The Great Depression and losing a part of our family, we also had the worst drought in anyone's memory. It was so terribly hot and dry. My dad would come in from the field for dinner. It was never lunch. And at night we ate supper. After dinner our family would go out on the porch, where it was a little bit cooler, so Dad could rest before he went back to the field. Mom and Dad had these same serious conversations that didn't make a bit of sense to me. We children would lay on the porch, on our backs, with our heads toward the outside edge of the porch, so we could watch the clouds. It was a sort of game. We had an abundance of clouds that summer, but NO rain. Maybe that's what our folks were talking about.

One question and one answer stand out in my memory. Dad would seriously say to Mom, "Ruth, look at all them big clouds. Ya' think it's gonna rain?"

My mom had a great way with words. She'd say, "How'm I supposed to know? But we can sit here and wait and see. Then we'll both know."

He never seemed to get angry with her, and I don't know why. I'm sure I would've.

And the rain didn't come, and the cornstalks began to wither up and die. The garden died. The grass died. We did pump water and saved the tomatoes. It seems to me now, we should've been made to water the rest of the garden. But maybe they were more concerned with the cotton, for it was our livelihood. You couldn't survive without cotton. I don't remember when it finally rained, but it did rain! It's funny. I remember praying for rain, but I don't remember when it came. But it finally came.

Another big thing stands out in my mind about 1931. My mother had lost track of her youngest brother. She hadn't heard a word from him since he'd returned from WWI. She had tried for years to find him. Communication wasn't too good in the 30's. We found out later that he'd been in Memphis, Tennessee all the time. That was about sixty or seventy miles from us. But understand, this was before people had phones and such. And fast cars had not been distributed to the poor folk at that time yet.

But finally an ad in our weekly paper got my uncle's attention, and he got in touch with us, and soon after paid us a visit. Wow! You should've seen his arrival. He came in a long, black shiny car that looked as long (to us country kids) as our cotton field. We kept circling this awesome car, looking it over real good, and Dad kept yelling at us not to touch it. We might get it dirty.

So I figured out one thing. My uncle must be somebody special to be riding around in this car. And all of those slick-looking characters that were with him. I figured my uncle must know Al Capone or someone like him, for these men were not cotton farmers. No way! They brought along an ice cream machine, ice and soda pop. Mom fried chicken and potatoes. She cooked dry beans (she did this everyday), she made biscuits and cornbread. We had fresh vegetables from the garden that was trying to die. Well, we had a feast and a great time. Everybody was so happy. My mother was happiest of all. I now understand it much better than I did then. This was the kind of a day that made one forget the dying garden and corn.

The cotton looked nearly done in, and the clouds still came up. But no rain came. And we rejoiced over what we had, and we kids didn't worry about tomorrow. We didn't reap a full crop of cotton, but we had some. And we didn't die or anything. And before you knew it, it was 1932.

And with 1932 comes another memorable event. The Cotton-Belt Railroad built a track right near our house. I remember watching the building of the roadbed, the laying of the ties, and then the nailing of the steel rails to the ties. It seemed to take forever, but finally the first train crept down the track.

And it happened like this. It was on a Saturday night, and we were all on our way home from town. Everybody went to town on Saturday night. It mattered not that no one had one cent in their pockets. That's just the way it was. So we were all walking home, down the railroad track because it was nearer. And to our great surprise, the first ever train comes up behind us, overtakes and eventually passes us. But not before I nearly had a heart attack!

We had been watching this atrocious thing for a very long time. (It was real slow.) But finally it caught us and there was no place to hide. Now you have to understand something. The light on the front of this thing had to be 40 feet tall and half that wide. It was a bright, piercing, penetrating and all encompassing tunnel of light you could not hide from. It was (to me) terrifying. We were accustomed to kerosene lights in our houses. This was awful.

So we talked ourselves into crawling down in the ditch and laying down on our faces until it passed us. But one thing we didn't plan on, couldn't have known, was the horrible noise that thing made. The whistle was nearly more than a body could stand, to say nothing of it's rumbling over the new unsettled roadbed. Then the huffing and the hissing and puffing and the spewing of steam. Now you must understand here, the parents did not lay down in the ditch! It was only us kids.

It sounded like (I imagined) a demon from hell. And as I lay there on the ground with my eyes squenched shut trying not to let the other kids know how terrified I was, I kept feeling these ripples of chill or thrill or whatever it was (It was pure fear, I'm certain now) running over my arms and down my back like a strong breeze going through a field of corn. I thought I would die, but I didn't. A human is a strong thing. We are survivors when it comes to imaginary trauma.

And now it's 1933. And later in the year another brother was born. What a great guy he was and indeed is. He came up much the same way I did, but with a lot more ambition, I guess. He worked his way through high school and enlisted in the Navy, got a good college education, and in a few years, worked his way up to "Director of Operations" for the International Holiday Inn Corporation. But that's another story.

The move we made in 1934 changed my life somewhat. It may have been the age I was, but it seemed like I went from being a kid to being a person. I guess it's called growing up. And though there was no big deal made about it, I saw that things were changing. Soon I began to notice a difference in boys and girls. I didn't say anything about it, I just knew.

There were no open discussions in my family about birds and bees. And through all of this, I was always intimidated by my sister who was quite a beauty. And I was always so plain, or even homely, and very shy also. So I acted mean and ugly to get my share of attention.

Now to breeze through 1935 with only a few outstanding incidences. I know I rebelled over a lie someone told me on the day of the school play in which I had a prominent part. I never did know who took my place in the program. My teacher withheld my report card until the beginning of the next term. I did pass to the ninth grade!

I do believe I fell in love for the very first time in that year. I know I was young, but it was real, for it lasted until that boy became a man of 74 years old. It was a pure, Elizabeth Barrett Browning kind of love. A veritable fairy tale kind of love. I loved this man until his death, sixty-two years after I met him. We both did marry someone else, but I always loved him. He had two children and I had seven. I didn't see him for the last fifty years of his life, but I loved him just the same. I wish people would make that kind of commitment in marriages now. But it would probably put divorce lawyers out of business or send them elsewhere looking for employment.

And now we greet 1936. This is the year I graduated from eighth grade. Big doings—A formal dress, high heels, the works. But with all this finery comes the realization that I am finished with school, and I'm devastated. My life is over, DONE! There's nothing left to live for. I loved school so much! So I sneaked off the stage, went into the cloakroom and cried myself sick. Finally I got mad and promised

71/MY LIFE IN BITS 'N' PIECES

myself I would (someday) go back to school. And the day came, forty years later. I graduated with honors in 1978, and then I felt vindicated. I was very happy. My seven children were in the audience screaming and carrying on fiercely. I think they were proud too.

1937 came in rather quietly, except for another flood. We had to move out of our house and into the house with our relatives up the road where it was drier. I remember my mother was pregnant with my youngest sister. Boy, was she a pain to put up with? I was going on sixteen years of age. My mother was thirty-nine years old that year, and she swore women died giving birth at forty. I suppose she was afraid. I know she was difficult to live with.

I had my last child at forty-three, and I'm not dead, and it's been thirty-six years. She has been a continual source of joy to me. Like I said, people can stand a lot of trauma.

We moved twice in 1938. It was a bad year. Late in the fall we moved all the way into another county. Forty miles away was like going to the moon. And there I fell in love again. This was a seventeen-year-old's desire for love. He was a good guy, and we had fun. And then he married his old sweetheart. This left me very lonely and probably contributed to my making the worst mistake of my lifetime. I let a bigamist talk me into marriage. I didn't know at the time.

And that was the start of nearly four years with a drunken bully who turned wife-beater at the blink of an eye. His dad and mom came from Texas for a visit, and his mom told me in secret that he had a family back home. I was young and very scared of him, but I did understand bigamist. So I weaseled my way out of that mess. And I did what all people did in my time. I went home to Mom and Dad.

Things were looking real bad. There was a war going on. I was back to hoeing cotton again. All the young men were either in Europe or the South Pacific. My own brother spent about four years in the South Pacific area—Guam, Wake, The Carolinas, The Mariannas and many islands whose names I've forgotten. It was a most dreadful time, and if we'd had TV and access to the news as we do now, we probably would have had more people with breakdowns and mental madness. I'm glad we did not know all then that we later learned.

But there is one bright spot in all the horror of WWII. I found and accepted the Lord as my Savior, and my life has never been the same since.

And now it's 1943, and I don't remember a lot except hard work. All of the young men were gone and that left all of the farming up to the women and kids and the older ones. And this was not a good thing. Finally the war was over, the boys that survived came home, but things were not the same. Many did not return at all. The ones that came home were a changed and mentally troubled group. They had seen and been a part of things we would never understand. It took them a long time to recover from the trauma they had experienced and many never got over it.

But to digress a bit. After I became a Christian my entire life took on new meaning, and I had some very happy years. Then in 1946 I got married. Woops! I think I've really done it this time. Now I've just signed a lifetime contract for lots and lots of trauma. But I learned to live with my poor decision. You always do, you know. I had been a Christian for a short time. I did not know much about "Be ye not unequally yoked together with unbelievers." I did understand, "until death do us part." So I set about doing the best I knew how.

In May of the following year (1947), I gave birth to my first son. And he was so precious. And, still is. I made him my life. I had nothing in common with his father. I already knew I had made a big mistake, but I was not free to leave (according to my understanding of the Bible). I did not believe in divorce, still don't. So I just went about trying to do the best job I could for my family. And in two years I gave birth to a beautiful little girl.

My husband was not lazy, but he wasted his money on alcohol and worse things, like evil females. So we often found ourselves in the house with his folks. And that was nerve-wracking for me with two small kids. Because we were in the house with other people, I was not left alone. So he had the freedom to run around with his single brother and act single. They ran with women, drank up every dime we both made in the field. He always made excuses for not having money for food and such. So I made little sunsuits and sundresses for my two babies out of flour sacks. Flour came in twenty-five pound sacks, and it was figured or flowered fabric. Everyone found a use for flour sacks.

My father and mother went to California in 1947. So in January of 1948 we sold or gave away everything we had and followed my folks West. It was a long trip on the Greyhound bus with a nine-month-old baby, but we did it. Out there I was totally happy. I had a great church with emphasis on the Holy Spirit and good teaching. I began to learn a few important things in the Bible. I was very happy and involved in church, and then my husband decided to go back to Arkansas (home) and pick some cotton.

So we loaded our car up like the Beverly Hillbillies and headed east. We were soon back in the house with relatives and picking cotton. I dragged my cotton sack up and down the rows of cotton with my fifteen-month-old baby on the sack. The cotton limbs would sometimes knock him off the sack and onto the dirt. I would get him back on the sack and start again. And to make this even worse, I was three months pregnant with all day sickness, not morning sickness.

Then my baby got diarrhea, and I had to leave him in our car at the end of the field. It was so very hot. And every time I went to the car to check on the baby, I found a dirty diaper and the flies swarming inside the car. They were crawling all over him because of the soiled diaper. He smelled so badly, my heart ached. I'd wash his face and hands, clean him up the best I could, but with diarrhea there was no keeping him clean. And my husband did not tell me once to take the child home and take care of him. But I reached a time when I could not look into his sick little eyes and my conscience would not tolerate the situation any longer. So I took him home, gave him a good bath and started to care for him as I ought. After I got him comfortable and asleep, I got on my knees by the bed and asked God to forgive me for the neglect my precious baby had suffered. God did forgive me, and the baby recovered. He is now fifty-three years old.

In the spring of 1949, we moved into the house with my sister and her rather large family. We were there when my little girl was born. After my daughter's arrival, we were a family of ten. We lived in a three-room house. Now this was a miserable time. My sister's husband was sick when we moved in with them. My brother-in-law had a form of epilepsy. He kept falling out, unconscious with seizures, so he didn't work much. My husband was out somewhere looking for the American dream. I was seven months pregnant and couldn't work in the field, so I was elected to keep the house and cook for the household. That left my sister to farm. She didn't get through hoeing the cotton till it was time to plow it. We had a very wet spring and summer in 1949, and so the grass never died. My sister was kept moving that grass into the row and then moving it out.

It was a very miserable year. And it got worse. My husband decided to go back where his folks lived. A bad move for me. My sister friends were poor, but her church friends gave me a baby shower so I did have a few clothes for my child. Now we were back at Blytheville near Roy's mom, and Roy is free to be single again. My babies and I were living in a homemade trailer house, picking cotton by day and staying alone at night.

My family life continued to deteriorate. My husband gave me no respect and, in turn, I could not respect him. I spoke respectfully to him, tried to be a good wife, but was very unhappy with the mess my life was in. I used to ask "why" a lot. I searched my heart and couldn't find any justification for the treatment I received. I now know that I made a poor choice, and I could not leave, so I was left to live with the results of my poor decision. I made it! A lot more hard work in 1950. Then in 1951 we came to Michigan. I loved it and still do!

Again I found a good church and Christian friends who assisted in trying to make my life easier. Here again the living was better. We soon owned a car. Then, eventually, we got another car. This was so I could take the family to church and not interfere with his means of travel. And now as I look back, I wonder why I had to hitchhike or bum a ride from the neighbors so much. Something does not compute.

By now I was thoroughly sick of the life I was living, and I couldn't speak kindly to him without much prayer. But I was still bound to him by an oath that I wasn't free to break. It was not the part about love, honor and obey; but rather the part about till death do us part.

So we continued to have babies, and in the summer of 1953, while I was waiting for my third child, my husband had an open affair with my next door neighbor. I was hurt and humiliated beyond words. Everyone knew of the affair. Now I was the object of everyone's pity. We lived in a one-room fruit picker's cabin, so nothing was hid. Things did not get better, so out of necessity I learned to lean heavily on the Lord just to keep my sanity. He, the Lord, never failed me.

Then in 1955, I had my fourth child. Another girl. I knew within the hour that something was wrong. I always breastfed my children, and when she nursed she made a terrible clicking noise. And the milk ran out of her nose. I'd never seen anything like it. I quickly asked the nurses about it; but they said nothing was wrong, the baby was just a little piggy. I knew better. Finally, as I was going home, my doctor told me she had a cleft pallet. I panicked and went to pieces until the doctor explained the simplicity of it.

77/MY LIFE IN BITS 'N' PIECES

Only her soft pallet was affected. It is usually accompanied by a "hair-lip," and sometimes other deformities. She had nothing that would show. It took some time for me to begin to realize how fortunate we were.

When she was thirteen months old, we took her to Grand Rapids for surgery. In a short time we nearly forgot there was ever a problem. She is now forty-five years old, well and healthy, and a lovely young woman.

Then in May of 1957, another baby girl arrived in our lives. I had spent the entire pregnancy wondering what would be wrong with this child. Nothing was wrong. She was perfect like all the others.

In 1960 another girl came. And in 1964 yet another. All were well and healthy and beautiful gifts from God. I was so blessed!

Then when the seventh one was six months old, their dad walked away, and I was left with seven small children and no visible means of support. Now we were realistically destitute. And, of course, I was left with a great deal of fear. But for the gentle grace of God?...

I tried to trust my family totally to God, but it was hard. And I knew it was not his fault. It was my choice. Some very hard years followed. My two oldest children rebelled against the kind of life they had to live, and against me. They quit attending church and began to run away. My big girl was the worst at running away. My big boy was getting in and out of jail at this time. I had no car in which to go looking for my daughter, and it nearly drove me mad. So many things can happen to a young girl out on the roads. Sometimes I left an unpredictable eleven-year-old boy to watch four small girls while I walked the streets calling my daughter's name. My heart broke as all I met with was defeat. I prayed and cried a lot in those days.

And while all this was going on, my church and other charitable institutions were feeding us and helping clothe us. Often the police would send me word (I had no phone) to come to the police station, and they would release my son into my custody. So I walked to the jail (I was seven months pregnant), got my son and started home. Then he'd suddenly remember he had to do something important before he went home. So I had a walk for absolutely nothing, and Roy was off and gone to who knows where. I would go home to my small children and wonder why I ever left them in the first place.

As one might expect, this son finally ended up in the county jail. Several times actually. Now he sent for me! He was scared! There was going to be a trial! They may give him six months! So my step-son takes me to the trial. And when the judge reminded Roy of all the times he'd given him another chance and of his continual spiral downward, he then gently but firmly sentenced him to eighteen months to fifteen years in Jackson Prison. Roy was sixteen years old at the sentencing. I went numb, I couldn't breathe. I thought I would die. Had it not been for my responsibilities to my six other children, I think I might've just checked out. But again God was faithful to me and saw me through some very bad times. I really leaned heavily on him. I had no choice!

I now skip over a lot of times and events. They were mostly bad anyway. The boy did his time and came home worse than when he left. He's a better criminal now, for he's been taught by Michigan's best.

Meanwhile, the oldest girl had continued her spiral, and you know which direction. She soon ended up in Girls' Training School. Now our major problem is: Who do we visit this Saturday?—A boy in prison and a girl in training school. I had to borrow a car and borrow money, too, and all of this to go see my children who would not behave. I loved them in spite of their waywardness, just like God loved me when I was so ugly in my sins.

So I continued to cry and pray a lot. There was no one to help, and no one I could go to for help, or even sympathy. So I got up daily and wondered when it would change. And I lived with the feeling that it would NEVER change. But now, after many years, it has changed. All of the children are grown up and doing well. Thank God!

And now I go to a night in November, 1966. I awaken with pounding on my backdoor. It's the police. I struggle to get awake, trying to understand what's happening. I know my son is in the county jail waiting to return to prison for his second time. My girl is in training school over by Adrian, Michigan. The younger kids are all in bed. So I'm very shocked to see cops at my door at three in the morning. They announced to me that my kids' father has been killed in a car accident in Arkansas. He was trying to outrun the police, drunk! His car had turned over five times.

Now here is the situation. I'm living off of $110.00 every two weeks from the state. I'm caring for five kids and myself, with some help from my church. There's not a penny left over, and I need to go to a funeral in Arkansas. Just one more trauma. I should be good at this by now. My church speedily got me $60.00, a car and a driver, and off we went to bury the father of my children. I got no pleasure from this. I did not rejoice! My two kids who were in jail couldn't even get out to attend their dad's funeral. We went, we came back home and the beat goes on.

I still had the nerve to hope things would get better. We lived in a sort of vacuum. Things couldn't get worse. We had surely hit the bottom. I grieved for my children's loss. I wet my pillow every night, after I got all the kids washed and in bed.

Then in 1967, with the help of some friends, I got a job. By now I was drawing social security from my husband's death. I thought I was rich. First, I bought us a car—a 1959 white Buick with red leather interior. I classed myself with the "Rockyfellows." I kept that job until January of 1969. Then I got a job with General Electric Company here in Holland, Michigan. I had bought a house and moved to Holland in January. Now I was doing well. After all of the trauma, I felt out of place. So I worked, paid for my home, kept the kids in school and even bought a new Camaro. Blue skies were everywhere now.

Son #1 was finally finished with prison. He married a fine girl, they were expecting my first grandchild, and all things were looking good. But how much goodness can a family endure, I ask you? To summarize: Father is dead. Mother has a good job, and we have a warm home. Brother is out of prison and doing well. But wait! Daughter #1 gets herself sent to prison. Oh yeah! Girls also go to prison.

By now you're probably wondering, where is this going? So I'll tell you. I'd just moved my family out of the country to the big city. We'd also arrived in the age of drugs, sex and rock & roll. I was ignorant of these things. I knew nothing about drugs. I had no defense against them. So son #2 got caught up in the middle of all this. Drugs were everywhere, for sale and to sell. The money was a dream come true for an unemployed schoolboy of sixteen or so. So son #2 found himself going to prison for selling just enough to supply himself in cocaine.

By now Daughter #1 had gone back for her second term in prison. Where I thought I had gotten us out of our misery, I found us back in it again. Good job, good home, new car, but in misery. It was like playing musical chairs. Who's in and who's out, and who'll be next?

But Son #2 only needed one time "in" to convince him. And, by the way, the four youngest girls spent so much of their young lives visiting in prisons they didn't feel the need to take up residence in one. Praise the Lord.

Now that time is long past. I often marvel at the way God brought us from there to here. I now have thirteen lovely grandchildren and three great-grandchildren. I still have my home. I finally retired my new car at eighteen years of age. My kids are all doing well and live near me. They are trying to make up for the past. I am happier than I ever dared hope I'd be. I look back and see my life as a tapestry. There are lots of dark threads in the picture, but through it all I see a bright thread. And I feel it is the hand of God that kept us through it all. I am glad!

Written on June 11, 1993

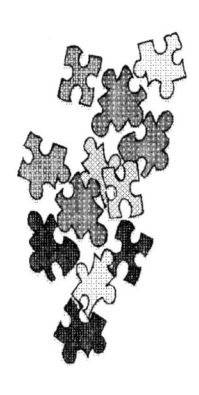

My Birth

I believe I am considered of average intelligence by most people who know me. My children must think I am of superior intelligence by the depth of some questions they ask me and, the number of questions. But to remember a lot about my birth would take the help of Superman and Lois, Yosemite Sam or maybe the Ninja Turtles.

Here are a few things I've been told. I was born to Bernie Bethel Underwood and Ruth Alice Nixon (2nd cousin to Richard Nixon) Underwood. I was born July 28, 1921, in Dunklin County, Missouri. I think Kennett, Missouri was the nearest town. There was a doctor who was called for (I think he came) and he wrote down the Statistics to have entered in the proper place among the other papers at the County Court House.

I'm told I weighed six or seven pounds. I had one sister when I arrived. Her name is Bonita Laverne. She was born April 26, 1919. Afterward, on August 10, 1924, my first brother arrived. Billy Burke was his name. On October 17, 1930, another brother was born. He died in July of 1931. His name was Bryce

Berniel. These two guys had the same initials as our father, but not the same name. They were, all three of them, B.B. Underwoods.

Then on October 12, 1933, another brother was born. His name is John Stanley. He is such a great person, but that's another story. Then on July 15, 1937, a sister was added to our family. Her name is Alice Elizabeth. And that is all the brothers and sisters.

As far as who was first to hear of my birth, I suppose it was my grandmother Underwood. She was an unlicensed mid-wife and was first to know about a lot of new babies. I'm sure I was born at home. Most every one was in those days. And it was a special day—my birthday. Much later, Jackie Kennedy Onassis was born on my birthday.

I know nothing of my mother's pregnancy and confinement. My mother had a theory and it was used for every part of life. It was this: anything from the chin down was TABOO! You did not look at it, touch it, talk about it or even admit that it was there. We didn't talk about dirty stuff in our home. As you may assume, I had some severe shocks ahead of me.

My dad was twenty-six years old when I was born and my mother was twenty-four. My dad was a very good carpenter, but with the Great Depression descending right on top of us—early in life—there was not much building going on in our part of the world. So Dad became a farmer. Cotton Farmer, if you please. My mother always stayed at home and took care of the house and children.

My grandmother lived with some of her children most of the time, and I remember when she stayed with us. At night, after everything was done for the day, we would all sit around the kerosene lamp, and she would read to us from a Zane Gray Book. And it was from one of these books that I was named. There was a character named Fay Larkin. My mother would not agree to the whole name, so they named me Fay Imogene.

I do not like my name, but who does? A schoolteacher shortened it to Gene when I was in the seventh grade. I liked that better. Still do.

I didn't know it, at the time but we were poor. And so very proud. I was born about two years after World War II. Warren G. Harding was president.

I'm told I was sick when I was born. Some people say I never got over it. A doctor was never consulted about it, and no name was given to it, but I guess I got over whatever it was!

My mother told me I was a very ugly baby. And I can believe that! She said later that she referred to the different colors I took on in my first two or three weeks of life. She also told me that she would throw a sheet over me when people came to see the new baby, hoping they wouldn't ask to see me. It's awfully hot in July in southern Missouri. No wonder I am like I am!

I grew up feeling very homely and unloved. But when I got saved at age twenty-three, I began to realize that I was a product of my parents but I was exactly what God had created. So today I feel good about myself. Not that I wouldn't change a few things, if I could. But I have a clean heart and soul and I am beautiful in the eyes of my Heavenly Father. What more could a person desire?

The Early Years

Since I am writing these events of my life in chapters or segments and I've already written about my birth, I'll try to write about my very early childhood memories, before I started school. Some of these things I remember very clearly and some things I've been told or heard told more than once by my parents.

I am told that we moved from the southeast corner of Missouri to the northeast corner of Arkansas when I was three years old or thereabouts. That would be in 1924. My first brother was born in August of that year. I don't remember the birth but I do remember where we lived.

My father was always a cotton farmer, but he would do any job available. How could you live in Mississippi County Arkansas and not work in cotton growing? Mississippi County grows more cotton per acre than any other place in the world. My dad was also a very fine carpenter and worked at this when a job could be had, which wasn't often. Thanks to the Great Depression. He often worked as an unpaid janitor at a nearby church. Sometimes he was the choir leader. I think he liked to be helpful any way he could.

And herein is my memory 'sparked' and it's very clear today. We were attending a summer revival meeting at this church. You couldn't miss a night! I remember needing to use the bathroom and this was before bathrooms had been invented. We had an outdoor toilet. Ever see one?

Now since I was only three, my very pregnant mother figured on cutting a corner, if possible. So she took me outside the open door of the church, away from the light that came streaming out of the door, settled me down behind a bush or shrub of some kind and told me to go for it! There probably was an outhouse out there in the dark somewhere, but my mom wasn't up to trekking across country in the dark looking for it.

But what she did not know was she had placed me on top of a pinching bug who took offense at the intrusion and grabbed my big toe. I was barefoot, of course. So that started a chain reaction. First, I let out a bloodcurdling scream. I began jumping up and down. My mom was trying to catch me to see what the problem was or whatever major malfunction I was suffering from. But in all this bouncing up and down, I suppose I finally beat this guy to death. Anyway, he let go of my big toe and after I had time to calm down a bit, life continued. I know now that this bug was a Hemiptera. No teeth. But at three I didn't know much about Bugology!

I always have clear memories of my father going to work early and coming home at noon for dinner. Then he went back to work and came home late for supper. I don't know who changed dinner to lunch and supper to dinner, but if I ever find out who did it, I'll tell him or her that you do not change sacred things.

Our home life was much the same every day, nothing special that a young child would remember sixty-five or seventy years later. But I do remember my baby brother clearly, when he was about a year old.

Shortly before I turned five, I started to school. You'd never think it now, but I was a very shy little kid. So shy that I could not ask permission to go to the "outhouse." It was like talking dirty!

Here I have to explain the schoolroom setup. It was a lot different from the schoolrooms of the 90's. We small children sat around a long, low table in low, red chairs. Well when a red gets real wet, it fades onto the calico dress that is pressed against it. And the red stain shows up a long way. Get the picture?

Kids are so cruel! They laughed at me all the way home while I cried the very same distance. All the way home. My mom had quite a job persuading me to go back the next day. But she won the argument and I'm so glad I let her win, for three days in kindergarten is not an awful lot of education.

Preschool Childhood

I don't remember much about 1925. Maybe we lived in the same house. I do remember where we lived in 1926 and 1927. I know we lived in the same house two years in a row. But that was rare. We usually moved every spring.

But I do remember two things that occurred in 1927. First of all, we had a flood. Nothing unusual about a flood in Arkansas in the spring, but I do remember it well. The other thing was a little more traumatic. My brother and I were playing on an old idle cultivator that was sitting along the side of our house. We found that by jumping as high as we could and exerting all our strength when we came down, we could pull the cultivator handles down, thus raising the cultivator tongue up in the air. We could hold the tongue up for as long as we could stay balanced on the handles. Anybody here ever seen a mule drawn, hand held, one row cultivator? No? WOW!

Well, one day our mother came flying around the house, saw what we were doing and screamed at us to "get off that thing before we got hurt." So we did. The tongue naturally fell straight down, hitting our mother on the top of her head, nearly breaking her neck! She suffered headaches the rest of her life, often telling us it was our fault. And I'm sure it was.

I remember hurting my brother rather badly in 1928. It wasn't my fault. I suppose we were arguing about something. I don't remember what, but my sister talked him (Billy) into rushing me. I was turning round and round in this empty room—with a one-gallon kerosene can in my hand. His head and the can's spout connected. The blood flew. And my sister threatened me with death, hell and destruction. My brother bled over everything and I cried! But looking on the bright side, he had a permanent, straight part in his hair all the days of his life.

As for the houses we lived in, they were mostly shacks. I don't know how we lived through the winters in them, but we did! From 1929 until 1933 we lived in better houses. I treasure the memory of those five years because of the houses.

And no, I never had a room to myself. And I was terribly afraid of the DARK! And the way I dealt with it was to cover my head with the quilt, and then it was even darker. I didn't think of that at the time!

Billy and I played with a red coaster wagon a lot. And I remember that some neighbor kids, Roy and Lorrene Farren, played with us a lot, too. We played church and took turns being the preacher. I think that was the first time I ever knew there was a difference in boys and girls. NOW, NOW, I only meant I had a crush on Roy. My first crush ever. He hated me!

My brother Billy died in 1988. We had a baby brother born in 1930. His name was Bryce. He died in 1931, not hardly a year old. Then in 1933 we had another baby boy born. His name was John Stanley.

He is now the head tax assessor for the state of Tennessee. Then in 1937 we had a baby girl born, Alice Elizabeth. Now, all of this did not happen before I was five years old.

As for feeling loved, I'm sure I did. I know we had food and clothing, of sorts, and two parents who were home every night. We had constancy. We were happy, and we didn't know we were poor.

As to accidents, I once stuck a pencil through the soft palette in my mouth. No, I didn't go to a hospital. I didn't even go to a doctor. I gargled peroxide a few times and ate soft food, and I got along just fine. If you don't believe me, just ask me!

As for pets, we mostly had dogs around. They weren't exactly pets. They were hunting dogs, but we did pet them. And we did have one little dog named Popeye, who was a pet and lived inside the house. He lived to be about fourteen years old. He was like a part of the family.

Life was slower in those days, more difficult for parents, but I wouldn't take anything for my memories of growing up in Arkansas during the good old Depression Days.

Where I've been, brought me to where I am now. But it's where I'm going that's exciting!!

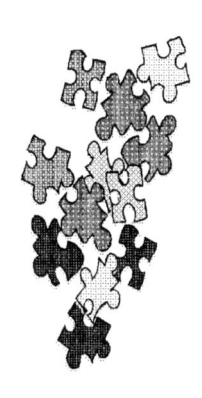

Elementary Years

I'm one who is never at a loss for words, but I'm not real sure where to start this segment of my story. But of course, I will start!

I'm not sure I remember my first day of school. I started shortly before I was five, so it's been a long time. I don't remember how far I lived from school, but I guarantee you I walked! My older sister was already in school, so I was not totally alone among strangers. Good thing too, for I was miserably shy! Anyone who knows me now will not be surprised to hear me say, I got over being shy.

We attended many country schools. I don't remember how many now. My father was a farmer, but we didn't own a farm. He worked for other people, so we moved a lot. In fact, when I remember the past, as I am doing now, I remember where we lived in all the different years. Some of my memories are based on where we lived at the time. As I was born in 1921, I only remember where we lived starting in 1924. My parents referred to 1924 and 1925 as, living on the

"Hays Place." In 1926 and 1927 we lived on "Section 12." In 1928 we lived on the "Robinson Place," and 1929 through 1933 it was the "Garner Place."

We always went to public school, and we always took homemade lunches. I remember a variety of goodies for lunch. The bread for our sandwiches was always the same, homemade biscuits. But the inside was different. Some days we had fried potatoes in our biscuit. Sometimes it was a fried egg or bacon or, here's the good one, fried okra.

We never had cookies, cakes, or candy. And when we were through eating, we went to the pump, stood in line and had a drink of water. I know that sounds primitive, but it wasn't bad. I'm now 72, and I have always had almost perfect health. So I guess it didn't hurt me. In fact, we didn't even know we were poor. We blended right in with the others. There was more equality then, I believe.

I remember how I loved geography. Three or four summers ago, I was in Boston, Massachusetts. And as I stood on Paul Revere Avenue and stared at the old North Church, I had a feeling that was close to a spiritual feeling. It seems like the cradle of civilization to me.

Now the question is about special interests or talents I might have had. I was a good scholar. I made good grades. I loved school. On time, every time, was my motto. And I was pretty good in athletics. I played some basketball, a little softball, but I was best in track and field sports. I was very fast on my feet. I won a lot of blue ribbons for racing, high jumping, broad jumping and such. I don't know what happened to me, I'm not nearly as fast as I once was!

Another thing I remember is a big hole in me—an empty spot of desire to be something that I had no chance of becoming. I needed recognition for something, anything. I wanted to be loved, and I know now that I was, but my parents didn't know how to express physical love. They thought if they did without food so we kids could be fed, that was love. And it was, but it was not what I needed so desperately. So, not until I was about 23 years old and gave my heart to the Lord, did I realize love in its fullness! My life changed here, and for the better, but that's another story!

Now, back to the earlier years. I never brought home a bad report card. I Always made good grades. I still have my eighth grade report card. It is old, brown, held together with Scotch tape, and it is still a treasure to me. My mom usually took care of all the little things in our home, but for some reason, my dad signed this card, and that makes it more of a treasure to me. My father was a great guy who never got a break in life, but he was still happy and go-lucky. He always made the best of a bad situation. He was also a great singer. We nearly always had a group that went around to fifth Sunday meetings connected to our church. I suppose if I had a talent, it would be singing or sports.

I remember a lot of my teachers from school. A Miss Dolly and a Mrs. Mary Mitchell. There were three sisters: Miss Elva, Miss Esther, and Miss Oma Hodges. None married! But the teacher who meant the most to me was Miss Lucille Stotts. She shortened my name from Imogene to gene. She showed me a lot of attention, which I needed for my self-esteem, and I just worshiped her! She even trained some of us sixth grade girls and took us to the big city and got us a thirty-minute spot to sing on the local radio. It was unheard of in my days, so you can imagine how overjoyed and proud I was. My head must have grown four sizes in a hurry.

As for other activities and games, we played marbles. We played jacks, pop-the whip, hopscotch and jumping rope. A lot of simple things, but it was fun. No bicycles or skates at my house!

Being hard working farm folk, we rested on Sunday. We did go to church when we lived close enough to walk. Sometimes my dad was song leader.

As for my siblings, I loved them a lot. I didn't know I had a choice. It was natural. But my first brother was so very special. As he was dying of cancer in 1988, he and I relived about sixty years of our lives. I wish I had tape-recorded our conversations, but I didn't think of it at the time. The pain of knowing he was dying was too much for me. Now, it's too late, but I remember!

I don't remember any trouble with any of my brothers or sisters, but this one was special.

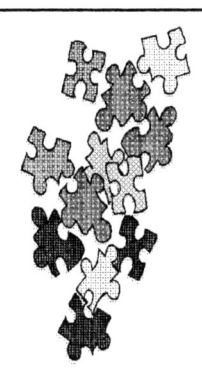

Teenage Years

I was not a very happy teenager, but neither was I a particularly unhappy one. In my day, a teenager did not "express" themselves as to their likes and dislikes, as they now do. We were under our parent's rule. We were grateful for food, clothing, heat, water and lights, even if it was a coal oil lamp, and other necessities of life. We didn't feel like outcasts because we did not have much! Nobody had much.

I loved my family. We got along well. I respected my mother, she was the brainy one. And I adored my father and my younger brother. My dad was a carpenter at a time when no one could afford to build a house, so he became a cotton farmer. So we got really good at barely getting by. We always had plenty of food, not too many clothes, but I think we looked just about like everybody else.

In our house, mama was the force to be reckoned with. Dad was always just a jolly Irishman! But there was no alcohol in or near our house. Mama would not permit it and dad didn't care enough about it to argue. And that was good thinking on his part, I most surely do believe!

As for rules in our home, we were taught that we could not lie or steal. We also had regular chores to do, but it was not a real strict regimen. Whoever was available did whatever needed to be done. And there was always Mama to tell us what needed to be done. It could be, "go bring in an armload of wood, go get a bucket of water, make the beds, sweep the floor or wash the dishes." Mama did most of the cooking. We went to the field in cotton hoeing and picking time. Everyone did! That was just the way it was. We didn't get paid for hoeing cotton, but we did get paid for picking. That was harvest time. It was just about all the pay we got for the whole year. Most of the men worked a half-day on Saturday, but never on Sunday.

The first job I ever had away form the farm was at a shirt factory. It was a no-brainer with no pay and no future. I hated it. I quit the job when I got married. I soon wished I was back in the shirt factory! Ha! Before I married I did not date very much. I was not pretty. I was not popular. I had absolutely no personality. Then I got saved in 1943 and I began to see myself through a totally different set of eyes. I had found the Lord, and He helped me find myself. I discovered that I was worth something to Him. I started to feel better about myself. I was no longer a self-conscious, homely young woman, but I was His child, and I loved it. I felt very special, and I still do.

As for entertainment in those years, we didn't have much. There was no money for anything but the barest necessities. I did see a few Western movies. I loved the Indians!

I always loved to dance. I learned to do the Charleston before I started to school. I always had rhythm, could do anything except tap or toe dance.

That's what we called ballet. I had very little training in music, but I could play an organ.

I learned how to drive my dad's old Chevy truck in 1941, but it was no fun. It didn't have any brakes on it. Not the best way to come up, but is wasn't all bad either! I have no regrets about my growing up years. Where I've been helps dictate where I'm going.

Written on February 21, 1996

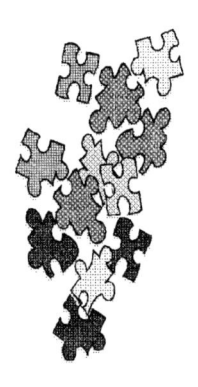

Young Adult Years

This one is not going to be easy to write. There are a lot of years here that absolutely nothing was happening. Nothing worth writing about.

I did graduate from the eighth grade in 1936 with no possibility of going any further in school. We lived about seven miles from the nearest high school and there were no busses, and not many cars. We certainly didn't have one! So my school days were over. I grieved over this, because I did love school so much. I literally wanted to know everything. I still do! I love learning!

I finished eighth grade and was ready for ninth grade. Little good it did me then, but I kept my report card and treasured it for all these years. (And it shows.) One of my reasons for treasuring it is because my father signed it. I don't remember why, for my mom usually did it. This card is 64 years old now.

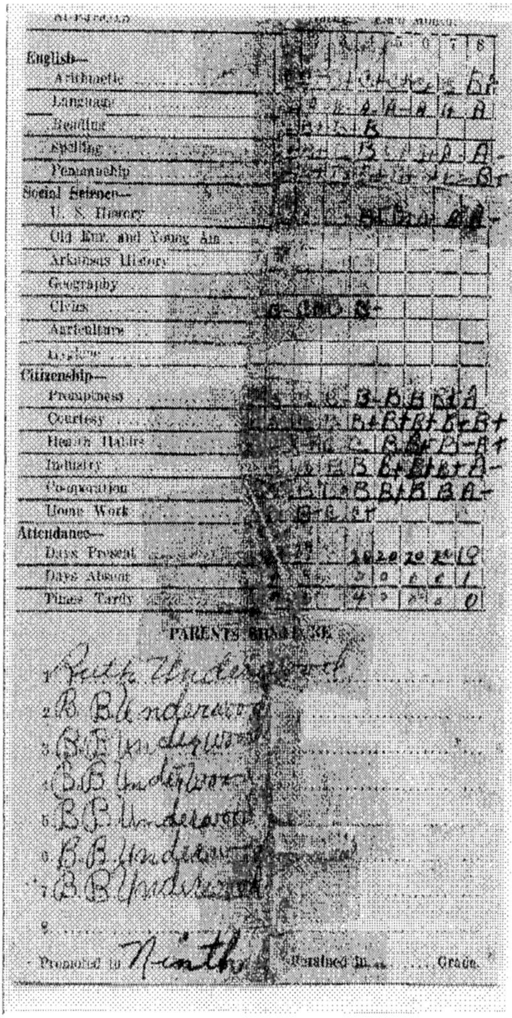

105/MY LIFE IN BITS 'N' PIECES

COMMENCEMENT EXERCISES

PAWHEEN SCHOOL

FRIDAY EVENING, MAY 15, 1936—EIGHT O'CLOCK

PROCESSIONAL

INVOCATION	REV. A. H. DeLANEY
SONG	"ENCHANTED GARDEN"
SALUTATORY	BLANCH METHENY
TOMORROW	FLORENCE LINDSEY
CLASS WILL	JUNIOR STONE
QUARTET	"SWEET AND LOW"
READING	WINFORD COBURN
CLASS ADDRESS	DR. L. A. TURNER
PARTING GIFT	ROZELLE ELLIS
DIPLOMAS	BRUCE CULP
ACCEPTANCE	RUBY UHLES
SONG	"HOME COMING"
VALEDICTORY	L. V. METHENY
BENEDICTION	MRS. MARY E. MITCHELL

CLASS FLOWER—RED ROSE

CLASS COLORS—RED AND WHITE

MOTTO—"MARCH IN STEP WITH PROGRESS"

CLASS ROLL

L. V. METHENY	WINFORD COBURN
JUNIOR STONE	RUBY UHLES
FLORENCE LINDSEY	VELMA WELLS
DAPHINE HAHN	ROZELLE ELLIS
DEVHUE HAMMOND	MOZELLE ELLIS
GEORGE PONDER	NYLINE JOHNSON
CORA BLOCKER	COMROZELLE DENSON
BLANCH METHENY	IMOGENE UNDERWOOD

After school there are not a lot of good memories for a while. Having been born in the country to country folk, I worked in the fields at the proper times. Nothing too hard, just a dull, no-way-out existence. We chopped cotton from April until the Fourth of July. Then we had a short break from the fields. Then in late August we started picking the cotton. Harvesting the crops might sound better. And that lasted until nearly the end of November. Sounds exciting, doesn't it?

And yes, during these years I dated a little. I was not very popular for several reasons. First of all, my sister, Bonita, two years my senior, was a very beautiful girl. I lived in her shadow! I was very homely and felt badly about my looks. I did not hate my sister, but I hated who I was. I felt every remark was made about me or was directly addressed to me, and always in an uncomplimentary fashion. I was very self-conscious, and so I'd always make sure I was absent when pictures were being made, and that sort of thing. Never out front! I was always behind!

Young people put so much stock in good looks and popularity, and I had neither. I tried to protect myself from rejection. I had a miserable teenage life. I'm sure I made it worse than what it actually was, but it was my life. I had to live it, and I hated it!

But I survived, praise the Lord! I now see myself as a new creature in Christ. I don't believe He sees me as ugly. I believe that when God sees me, He just sees another one of His children and He loves me. And I am very happy about that.

We did go to church during some of these younger years, but not for the right reasons, only that there was nowhere else to go. It was school, church, and fields.

And once again, my sister shined in church. She also shined in school. She shined with our parents too. I guess you could say she was a "shiny girl!" Very hard act to follow. I always felt second best—kind of in her shadow. My parents did not know how to bestow more attention on the unlovely child. They probably didn't even know how I felt about myself!

But you know what? I would not trade one day of my life for all of her days. This sister has become a miserable, bitter, self-pitying old woman who is soured on life! She does now know the Lord except with head knowledge. She blames everybody for everything that ever happened to her, and she lives in absolute misery. Her life has not been good. No, I would not trade places with her at all. I love every day of my life now!

But one good thing about these younger years, my father was from a musical family. Members of our family always had a duet, a trio or a quartet of singers that performed at social functions, such as church fifth Sunday meetings and Tri-County gatherings. And on these occasions I got to be #1 with my dad. My sister did not care to sing. I was singing harmony with my dad before I had any idea why. First off, my voice was always so low I couldn't get "up there" where he was, so I dropped down lower and still made it sound good.

I remember the first time he noticed it. I was six years old. We used to sit up a night around the heater in the dark after the chores were done for the day, and we would sing! And my dad, having an ear for this sort of thing, heard me. I remember hearing him say to my mom, "Ruth, who was that?" I kept ever so quiet, thinking I had done something wrong.

But as time went on and I grew bolder, I continued to sing harmony with him. He was proud and let me know it. Also I began to get a lot of attention from his singing friends, and I valued it. I was finally somebody on my own rights, with a little bit of personality. So my father and I embarked on a long career of singing Gospel music. He even taught me the first ten rudiments of music.

The Stamps Baxter Music Company used to send my dad four new songbooks at the beginning of each new year. We loved these books, but we also knew our work had just begun. We had to learn all the new songs in the book, which we did. We had learned the shaped notes. Dad was a teacher, of sorts.

And so, my life took on a new dimension. We went places! People knew us! We were somebody, and I loved it. This singing together continued throughout my life until my dad grew too old and sick to sing, and I had too many children to sing with him. My dad had lung cancer later in life, and afterwards he didn't have enough air to be able to sing. I think the last attempt we made to sing was in 1955. I still love to sing.

But my life was not all sadness and gloom. Our parents instilled some values in us, even if they were not what I call Christians. These were values that would go through life with us. Our parents were very adamant about truthfulness and honesty. Call it our daily diet! And you better not get caught straying from the path. And to my knowledge, there is not a thief or a liar in the Underwood Family. That was my maiden name.

Just a quick P.S. to this chapter. The school situation changed also. When I was 57 years old, I graduated from Holland High school with top honors! But that is another chapter in my life...

Now I have a real-life, honest-to-goodness, full-sized, red-backed diploma to add to my little eighth grade report card and my G.E.D. certificate. I call these things "parts of my collection." So, I guess these things are as good as a lot of other things I collect, like baseball paraphernalia!

And I am very happy in the place I am in now.

Lauds Adult Graduates

The seventh annual Holland Adult High School Completion commencement Wednesday night was the climax of a dream come true for the 54 graduates and 24 GED students.

About 300 guests attended the ceremonies that were held in the Holland High School Auditorium Performing Arts Building.

Speaker for the commencement was Dr. Kenneth Vaught, associate director of the Community Education Development Center, Western Michigan University.

Dr. Vaught said the graduates should recognize they are a new breed who represent an increasing number of adults completing high school and higher education.

Adults have an advantage over younger students, he said, because of their experience and background, their better idea of what they want to learn and because they are more motivated.

Peter Roon, assistant superintendent of West Ottawa Public Schools congratulated the graduates on going through valleys to reach a "mountain peak experience."

Awards were presented to Fay Key, graduate with the best overall grade point average, Lynn Duncan for best GED test score and to teachers Don Larsen and Wayne Nyboer as outstanding teachers. The outstanding teacher awards were voted by the students.

Fay Key, 31 East 17th St., Holland, finished her two years of high school completion with all A's except for two B's and one C.

Employed at General Electric, Mrs. Key said she completed high school "for pride," not because she wanted a different job.

When she graduated from the eighth grade during the Depression with no chance to go onto high school, she promised herself that someday she would have a high school diploma.

Now, Mrs. Key plans to attend Grand Valley college this fall, taking creative writing and psychology.

"Not many good things have come my way," she said. "This is one of the biggest things in my life."

110/MY LIFE IN BITS 'N' PIECES

THE TOPS — The two top teachers and two top students in Holland Community Education were honored Wednesday night at Holland High School. Wayne Nyboer (left) and Don Larsen (back) were voted top teachers by the students. Fay Imogene Key (right) had the highest grade point average in the high school diploma program. No pictured is Lynn Duncan who had the highest GED score. She was unable to attend the graduation ceremonies.
(Sentinel Photo By Deb Torres)

Articles on pages 109 and 110 are from the Holland Sentinel, reprinted here with permission

Holland High School

This Certifies That

Fay Imogene Key

has satisfactorily completed the Course of Study prescribed by the Holland High School and is therefore awarded this

Diploma

Given under our hands and Seal at Holland, Michigan, this month of June, one thousand nine hundred seventy-eight.

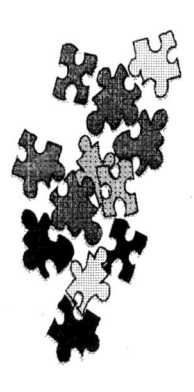

Flashbacks

I awoke this morning with flashes of memory washing over me, suddenly coming back down that long dim tunnel of near forgetfulness. Great memories! Precious People! Good times, and some that aren't so good! And it is about a time in 1945 that I am thinking. But to set this time up and make it understandable, I have to go back to another day and another time.

I had gotten married in 1940. This lasted about four years (I've written about this in another chapter of this story). It did come to an abrupt stop! And now, I'm living back at home with my parents. Some may wonder why. Well, I'll tell you. That's just the way it was done in my day and time.

A person from a failed marriage (no matter why it failed), whether a spouse died or just ran away or whatever the reason might be, just went home. They were then integrated back into the life of the family. They took on some of the chores or work and again became a working part of the family they had left.

Father and mother were still the joint-heads of the family. They still made the rules and decisions. And, to think about it, all of this was before welfare had become a national disgrace (as I see it), and a terrible drain on the Unites States Government. I think, if the congressional spending and welfare could be brought in line, we could balance our deficit.

In my day, a young women did not get her own apartment, have a decent car, have various boyfriends and lots of babies; and the welfare pay for all of it for her. And it pays pretty good too!!

But this episode was not meant to be about the faults and failures of welfare. My flash of memory had to do with a cousin of mine, who also lived at home with me in my father's house. She was my father's brother's daughter, Jewel Underwood. She was a few years younger than myself.

I was about twenty-four years old and Jewel was about nineteen. We worked all week in the cotton fields. Cotton farming is hot hard work, but a very necessary thing in our part of the world. So we did what had to be done and didn't even know we could complain.

So in July in Arkansas with the temperature at 98 degrees or more, we all went to the field to hoe cotton. My dad plowed the middles between the rows, and that's how we encouraged the cotton plants to produce and make us some money. Sounds simple, don't it?

But here are some more small details. First, we went to the field bare-foot, and about 11 o'clock till 4 p.m., the soil was almost unbearable to our feet. I suppose we had shoes of some kind to work in. I don't know why we didn't wear them!

But I remember my cousin and I reaching as far as we could, ahead of ourselves, and digging a hole to step into to keep from getting burned or blistered feet!

Now isn't it odd that I would wake up on December 1, 1993, remembering little holes I dug in the hot soil in a cotton field in Arkansas back in June of 45? Do you suppose I'm weird or something?

This cousin married her childhood sweetheart later and had a good life. She had three lonely red-haired children. They went to live in Texas until the husband died. Then she and her kids moved back home and, to this day, she lives on the Arkansas-Missouri state line. I saw her in 1989 at our family reunion. We had a great time remembering when.

I do thank my God always for my memory for, so often, I go back without a ticket or an invitation and visit with some dear people from long ago. And I love it!

Do You Believe in Angels?

My marvelous memory takes me back to 1949, and I remember a story you may or may not believe. But I believe it, and I guess that's all that really matters.

But, to digress a bit: My parents, my youngest brother and sister, my brother Billy, his wife and baby had gone to California in 1947. So in January of '48 my husband, our baby and I went to California also.

I loved the country, would have stayed there forever had I been in charge of our destinies. But in early August of that same year, my man got this great longing to go home. So we packed up our few belongings, loaded our '29 Model-A Ford to the max and headed for Arkansas. That was home! I wish you could have seen this extended family as they headed for home. I'm so glad God watches over babies and fools, for we were a car full of such. There was Billy, Lucille, baby Nikki, Roy Sr., Roy Jr. and I, my teenage brother, Stanley, all on a mission impossible or nearly.

We were five adults, two babies and everything we owned all stacked, packed and crammed in this very small car. We had four tires stacked on the back and two five-gallon cans of water tied on the fenders. Yes, cars used to have fenders! We were glad, too, for people had told us that most cars got overheated going over the great divide high up in the Rocky Mountains. Our car ran perfectly all the way home. I think God saw our ignorance and just sort of watched for us. We went around many newer cars that were parked with boiling radiators. We got to Arkansas some four days later and still had all of our California water in our cans!

The western United States is so beautiful. You'd have to see it to believe it. It is just breathtaking to see the Mountains pushing up, up through the clouds and still straining to touch the sky, always with snow on the highest peaks. Then there's the evergreen trees, the creeks, rock-strewn, the valleys, box canyons. We don't have many evergreens in Arkansas where I came from. Therefore I love green trees a lot.

It is not uncommon to see eagles soaring about or even a condor. Elk, deer, moose and even bear are quite common. No angels, yet! So we went home, left all of this beauty and went to the delta lands of northeastern Arkansas to pick cotton. There are no words to express my disgust. I hated all of it now, more than ever before!

About this time I discover I am pregnant. Not exactly good timing, but timing had absolutely nothing to do with it. And to further confuse the issue and make the situation almost totally unbearable, my husband developed a great dislike for married, pregnant women. He decided he liked younger, prettier girls. So we picked cotton by day, and he ran the streets by night from bar to bar.

We bought a homemade trailer house. So I sat home at nights, my baby and I alone, and I thought long and hard about "not being unequally yoked together with unbelievers." It took on a totally different meaning. "Till death do us part" started to loom large on my horizon! I was married in '46 and my husband died in '66. A very long time! No angel, yet!

In early spring of '49 we got the message that our Dad was very ill in California. No one had a dime except my brother, Bill, who was getting his very last unemployment check from the Navy. So he left wife and child with me, took his $40.00 check and started for the West Coast to help Mom take care of Dad.

He bought a bus ticked for as far as $40.00 would take him. I think he got somewhere in New Mexico. There he took off, with no food, no smokes, no nothing, walking into the sunset, scared to death, but he had to go.

I can't remember the tale word for word, only the gist of it. He walked until he felt he couldn't go any farther. There he would sit down by the roadside and rest for a while. Sometimes he would awaken and realize he had been asleep. Part of this trip was through desert country, no trees or shade, but he walked on. Sometimes he slept, but always being led by his heart, westward! And always being torn between wife and child and parents. He remembered, once or twice, being picked up and riding for a few miles and then being told they were going north or south. And he was going west. And he grew steadily weaker from having nothing to eat.

Eventually he was in Los Angeles, and no one picks up hitchhikers in a city, and it's 35 or 40 miles through this city, south to north. So on he goes, fading in and out of consciousness, mostly unaware of time or place, wondering if it had all been for naught. Then it happened! Out of an alley a man stepped up to my brother and addressed him thusly, "Brother, you look like you could use a little help." And all the time this man kept his head down and his face in the shadows.

My brother first thought he was dreaming, or worse, that he was hallucinating. Then he realized he was awake and started to try to explain his situation. This man said he was there to help, so he took money out of his pocket and pressed it into Billy's hand and started to leave. Billy thanked him and asked for his name and address saying he would send the money back as soon as he got to Dad's house. The stranger said, "I can't do that, but, if you ever see me again, you will know me!" Then he faded into the darkness quickly.

In later years my brother related this story a few times, and he seemed to grieve because he couldn't repay this man who evidently had saved his life. I have no earthly explanation for this incident, except Lucille and I were earnestly praying for his safety on the trip. Any of you who know Lucille, must know that she knows how to get in touch with God. She was just a young Christian at this time, but it didn't take her long to understand the dynamics of prayer.

Years passed. Now it is the fall of '87, and Billy has been told he has cancer with three to six months to live. He had never given his life to the Lord, but during these painful months, he finally did, due to good folks ministering the Gospel to him from our church.

I firmly believe he finally came face to face with the man who had saved his life many, many years ago in California in 1949. I can hear the man say to Billy, "Your debt has been paid in full. I know, for I paid it myself."

Billy died in April of '88, a long time after '49. God's patience is wonderful, isn't it?

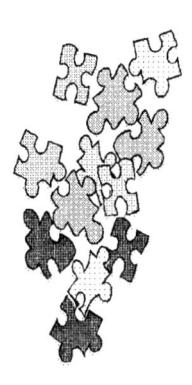

The Good, The Bad and The Ugly!

This will not be easy to write, but I believe it is necessary! I have struggled with this part of my life for a very long time. I was of the opinion that it should be buried and forgotten, if possible. But since I've not been able to do that, since it has a way of coming back to trouble me occasionally, maybe writing about it will serve, in a sense, like an exorcism. We'll see!

And now to digress, once more. As I have previously written, I was born to good, honest, law-abiding parents. Though they were not what we now call born again Christians, they had very strict ideas about morals. We were taught truthfulness and honesty. Sexual morals were not talked about, they were just understood. I don't say this to boast but, never once, before I was married at the age of nineteen, was I even slightly tempted to give in to a young man's "If you love me you would..." approach. I didn't struggle with the question "Should I or should I not?" I just knew it wasn't right...end of argument.

I don't believe promiscuity was as popular in those days as it is now. But I was warned about the bad girls. I was not totally left in the dark. But I did spend time wondering what it meant to be BAD. HA! I was very dumb, then.

As I've labeled this chapter about my life "The Good, the Bad and the Very Ugly", I suppose these young, innocent and dumb years are the "Good" ones. I don't think it is wrong to be dumb about some things. I remain proud of my upbringing. I even tried to bring my own seven children up with the same innocence and same values, but I'm afraid I didn't succeed. More later!

There's not a lot to be said about the "Bad" years, as it only related to the economic situation the U.S.A. was in when I was young. The Great Depression Era! There was no money. We farmed and just barely eeked out an existence, not a living. But as I look back, it wasn't so bad. My mother always raised chickens so we had eggs (some of the time), we also had young frying chickens to eat in the spring and summer. We had a garden, which we really appreciated. All that fresh, green stuff after a long winter of dried beans, fried potatoes and biscuits or corn bread. Sounds good, don't it?

And then, my dad always raised and fattened a big hog every year. And at the right time of the year (about first frost in November), he killed this animal and cured it with salt. So, as long as it lasted, we had bacon, ham, shoulder and all of the other lesser parts that were sooo good. I remember making sausage. It was a big messy, greasy job that might last two or three days. We used a hand grinder and it was slow, even though the entire family got in on the act.

We usually owned one milk cow too. So we had milk and butter a good part of the year. I only remember one cow, and she was a part of the family. Her name was Babe.

So now I've partially covered the "Good" and the "Bad." And I find that I no longer can ignore the "Ugly!"

I have spent a lot of time trying to figure out why I allowed myself to fall into this pit. In fact, actually, I didn't fall into the pit, I dug the pit. I even remember how proud I was of the pit. It was the nearest thing to love that I had ever known. I speak of physical love!

How to start? Where to begin? At the beginning, I suppose! Okay?

When I was very young (in my early teens), I fell in love with a young man. I'm sure it was mostly an emotional love. There were no thoughts of sex (may I use that word?), just Elizabeth Barrett Brownings kind of love! It was pure and precious, and I still cherish the memory of my first love.

At nineteen I married a man who was already married. You've heard of bigamy, haven't you? Read on....

I stayed in this intolerable situation for four years (I don't know why), then I left him. It was a case of all sex and no love. Then, when I was twenty-five, I married the father of my seven children. And there began eighteen years of **special misery**; very little sex, and no love on my part, nor on his, I suspect.

Then he walked away, leaving me and seven children; and that was better than having him with us. This was in '64.

In '69 I bought my house and moved to Holland. Now we're getting close to the ugly! Meanwhile I have completely back-slidden, and I'm going to bars just to be with people. My kids are "doing their thing," or most of them are, and I'm beginning to be real lonely. At least, that's what I told myself. Then late in '69, I met and fell madly in love with a man. On our first date, he told me about his wife and family. Was I shocked? No! I was crazy in love! After a few dates, I was beyond the point of "no return." I told you it was ugly. So began nine years of living at the highest peak of ecstasy and falling into the lowest pit of despair, for he could not always be with me.

And when he was not with me and he was not at his home (I checked), then I would become frantic. I knew, well, what he was doing to his wife, with me; and I felt sure he would not hesitate to do the same to me with someone else. And therein was a great deal of my punishment.

I confided in certain friends of mine at work. There was no shame in me. They said they could tell when he had been by my house. They said it showed. My kids knew all about it... They all knew I was in love for the very first time. They didn't agree with what was happening, but they loved me and were glad I was happy, WHEN I was happy! And when I was in the depths of despair, they wanted to look him up and kill him.

Now in this relationship there was both sex and love, for, believe me, he did love me. But never the way I loved him. And believe it or not, he loved his wife. I do not understand his infidelity. She was always number one. I knew it and even respected it.

I always told him I'd be number two for as long as we both lived, but I'd never knowingly be number three or four. So, after nine years, I saw him with another woman, and I went crazy and cracked their heads together real hard and tried to maim them. He overpowered me and brought the anger in me to a halt. The police asked me to leave the building and, having no other recourse, I left.

But this was not the end. I now felt shame but evidently not enough. After some time he came back with a real sorry excuse, and you know what? I went for it! Not that I was ever comfortable again with him, but he was like a cancer to me. There was no way to get him out of my system.

Then came the last time! I had not planned what happened. I didn't want to say it, but I found myself sitting at the foot of my bed, like Buddha, and saying words with no thought or effort. They just seemed to issue forth. Ha! He knew something was wrong so he said, "Okay, Gene, tell me what's wrong." And I said, "What you have to offer me is no longer acceptable." Classic last words!

Then started years of grief, shame and loneliness as I've never known before. I cried a lot. I drank some. I wrote lots of letters to him that I never meant to send. I still have them. Maybe I should burn them, but so far I've never been able to part from them.

I've not seen a glimpse of him in these last thirteen or fourteen years. I don't want to see him! I do see some of his kids from time to time at the Fourth of July fireworks and things of that nature.

His wife and children were nice people, and I loved them more than they knew, and for a reason they never understood.

Then my brother got fatally ill with cancer and through that I came back to the Lord. I repented with many tears, and finally found peace in Christ. He forgave me, but it took years for me to forgive myself.

After a long time, Romans 8:1 became a reality for me, and I've felt much better about myself ever since.

So now, I know the past is exactly that, past! My sins are covered with the blood of Christ Jesus. I am a new creature in Him and I am loving myself again and enjoying every day of my life.

When I think of this "Ugly" time in my life, I quickly ask the Lord to wipe it from my thoughts and not let me dwell on it. My one hope is, that having confessed it and written it down on paper, I can finally put it to rest. Bury it!

It was the best of times and, by far, the worst of times.

Earthquakes in Diverse Places

I don't know what brought this thought to my mind, but suddenly I'm thinking of earthquakes in diverse places (Matthew 24:7). And at the risk of seeming selfish or worse, I'm glad they are in diverse places and not in Michigan! It is not a thing the normal person would look forward to, not Michiganders, not Californians, and not even the diverse people.

After having watched the news on TV for several days and seeing all this mass of lost, scared, disoriented, terrified and hurting humanity, our hearts go out to them. I found myself glued to the set, I couldn't leave. I went into tears on several occasions, wishing there were a way I could help them, but not knowing how.

Now, I'm not totally ignorant of disasters and their aftereffects on people. Although I've never suffered the loss of one of my children (thank the Lord!), and I've never had all my earthly possessions destroyed by fire, I have suffered the loss of everything I owned to a flood. And more than once! So I do know the feelings of helplessness and near hopelessness.

I found myself praying for the different faces that caught my attention on the TV screen. I wondered if they were saved. I wondered if they knew they could draw strength from the Lord! I wondered if they were aware of the scriptures that speak of earthquakes.

Now we know that earthquakes are not a strange thing in California. I've often wondered why everybody in that state don't just pack up and move east. But I guess that just isn't feasible, is it? The same way that people don't move away from flood areas.

We know there are numerous earthquake faults in the U.S., and most of them are on the West Coast. The seismologists, who spend their lives studying this type of phenomenon, have learned an awful lot about earthquakes. They have even given names to some of the better-known faults. They are also able to know a little about when and where the next earthquake will be. They can even guess at the size of it and try to determine how much damage it may cause. And this is all due to the modern machinery they have to work with and their seismographic statistics.

But scientists are rarely able to warn people ahead of time, so they can evacuate troubled areas. Or maybe they just don't believe it will happen this time. But it seems they always get caught unprepared, like this latest catastrophe. People were dug out of their collapsed homes and apartments and didn't even realize they were naked until they were in the streets.

The quake occurred at 4:20 a.m., and they were all in bed. So this speaks to me of "in an hour when you think not—your Lord cometh"—or the trouble cometh or the unexpected cometh. This may not be a proper comparison, but it should cause us all to think of the seriousness of the Lord's imminent return.

So, while most of us cannot do anything to alleviate the suffering of the quake victims in California, we should let it awaken and stir us to where we are in the grand scheme of things in the world today.

The Bible tells us to be awake and prepared for the Lords coming. Matthew 24:36 tells us, He will come in an hour that no man knoweth. Verse 44 says, "In an hour when you think not." The Lord admonishes us to keep our lamps trimmed and burning bright and to have an extra supply of oil in our possession in case we have to wait longer than we expect. Matthew 24:1-13 says, "Watch, for ye know not the hour."

I don't know if there is any correlation between the "Great Quake of '94" and the return of the Lord, but I seem to find some likeness in the two things. One thing I know, if the good man (in California) had known in what hour the earth would quake, he would have gone to bed with his longhandles on or at least his Hanes His Way! This man, and all the others also, resided on the exact spot where the earth chose to quake. But knowing this, they failed to be prepared. Probably most of then knew there are two places in the whole world where 95% of all quakes occur, the Pacific Belt and the Mediterranean Belt. Most people know this, but it didn't cause them to be prepared, did it?

But here is the difference, and possibly a great advantage to us who claim to be awaiting the Second Coming of the Lord. We have a greater seismologist, who has not only told us, but has had it written down for us in the Holy Bible. Our instructions are very clear. It is said, "The way is so plain that a wayfaring man, though a fool, could not err therein."

So we can't plead ignorance, we can't say we didn't know where the **fault** was. For if there is a **fault,** it is ours for not studying the Word and getting ready to go, suddenly and without forewarning, to be with the Lord.

Even if the call comes at midnight!

Racing Cars for Fun

I remember a season when my family's entire efforts were spent on racing cars and motorcycles. My oldest son, Roy, started driving for a friend of his. Pretty soon the "bug" got him, and he started to build his own racecar. It was not built for looks, but for power. The body was strictly secondary. The engine was the principal part. He started racing at Hartford, Michigan, on an oval track.

We screamed, yelled and carried on like the people who were winning first, second and third place and taking the money home. It was family fun and it was great excitement. We planned our lives around the Saturday night races. We bought programs, and I personally chased drivers all over the place to get their autographs. Some of those guys went on to race in Nascar races. Butch Miller, for one, and Johnny Benson for another. Then the drag race "bug" got my son, and we began going to the 131 Speedway Racetrack. This went on for several years. I love the drag races much better than the oval track races.

We used to pack two or three ice chests with food and drinks to take to the race, for we knew we would be there till midnight before we would come home. Food bought at the track ran into a lot of money, so we took our own. But I guess money was the reason we never did get into big-time racing. We didn't have the money, and it is an expensive hobby. My son was a great driver, and he got a lot of recognition. His qualifying times were usually good, but someone else always took the money home. You need good sponsors!

Well, he did win a little, but you have to win a lot to be able to continue racing, or have a lot of money coming in from somewhere else. We didn't have that unlimited flow of cash, so eventually he became discouraged and we quit competing.

He still has his car and his dream! He always thinks there will be a time when he can race, again. It is stored away in this garage, and when he is not working on other people's cars, he finds time to do a little bit more to the racecar.

I think dreams are great and I'm real glad our family had this particular time of unity. We do not always agree on most things.

We met a lot of people who were, and still are, famous in Stock Car Racing. We especially loved "Big Daddy Don Garlitt" (see picture at left). I guess most race fanatics do.

I also had to admire Shirley "Cha Cha" Muldowney (see picture at right), the first female to race against males in that particular class. She even beat Garlitt, at least one year.

I don't know how Shirley is doing now, and I understand there are more women in racing now! At least one more.

We still follow racing, still love it. I have one girl who goes over near Jackson, Michigan a couple of times a year to the big-time races. A Dale Earnhart fan! So Dale Earnhart is a big name in our house. With my family it's not just big names, it's just for the fun and competition of racing.

Roy Key's second racecar

136/MY LIFE IN BITS 'N' PIECES

When the family is not oval track racing, they do mud running. My son, Billy, was closely connected with a big-time mud runner. The name of the machine was "Light-Flight." The owner is Ray Wells of Holland, Michigan. He races internationally. My son was part of the crew of mechanics that kept the mud runner running.

Craig Meyer and Dale VerHey, part of the racing team

137/MY LIFE IN BITS 'N' PIECES

Last, but not least, my number one granddaughter was a runner all through school—including college. So I guess racing is in our blood. I like the challenge of getting off the line first!

My daughter, Molodi "Mel" mud running

My son, Billy, with "Sloppy Joe"

The Gifts God Gives Us

I suppose the gifts we treasure most are sight, hearing, smell, taste, touch and so on. But the one I'm impressed with is memory, which covers all of the above mentioned gifts. All one needs is a new sight, sound, odor, taste or any of the already named gifts and our memory is jogged and the past becomes the present once more. It all works like a computer. Touch the right button and you get the answer.

I was talking to my doctor a few months ago, and he suggested I try my hand at writing. Of course, I told him I had no formal training or education. But he said, "You have something much better, you have a lifetime of experience. So write!"

I guess I let him talk me into it, for this is my third attempt. I know I'll never be an Edgar Alan Poe or a Jack London, but maybe somebody will enjoy what I have to say. I couldn't ask for or expect more.

So now I'm thinking, using this marvelous memory, of a night in May of 1936. There is a graduation class of about twenty young, back-woodsy, cotton-picking kids thirteen to sixteen years old. The young men wearing suits (I can't imagine where they borrowed them), and the girls are wearing formal dresses and high heels, their very first ones, I'm sure.

I remember so very well, wobbling down the aisle to the beat of Pomp and Circumstances and standing, front row, before my parents and the entire neighborhood. Was I proud? You bet! Happy? Ecstatic! The future was mine!

And then as the program progressed, I became aware of the fact that this was my last night of school. I'm sure I had always known it but it had never seemed so final. The nearest high school was seven miles away. There were no busses, not many cars, and we certainly didn't own one. This was the end! The thought broke my heart. So, instead of remaining on stage for the congratulations of the people, I sneaked into the cloak room, hung myself up on a coat hanger and commenced to wail, long and loud. I told that wall (after I had cried myself sick and my pain turned to anger) in no uncertain terms that I would go to high school one day!

Ten years came and went by with not much happening. Then in 1946 I married. From then till my husband left us in 1964, I had seven children. With each birth our life became harder, financially. When my husband finally left, my last baby was six months old. Survival began to be my only thought. I don't know if we could have made it, had it not been for the faithfulness of the Lord.

Then, after a lot of years, I got my chance to go back to school. This was in 1976, only forty years since I had finished eighth grade in 1936.

Thank the Lord for His faithfulness and my determination to learn.

141/MY LIFE IN BITS 'N' PIECES

I went to school at night. I was working days at General Electric Company. It took me two and a half years to earn my real life, honest-to-goodness High School Diploma from Holland High School. And I was only fifty-seven years old!

I loved every minute of the time spent in classrooms. I had a great time doing it! Maybe I even encouraged some other adults to go for a diploma. Friends asked me if it wasn't much harder to learn after having been out of school so long. I said, "No," for I didn't find it hard at all. I still have my very good memory that God gave me. Now, do I end this?

I still have my eighth grade report card. I'm still proud of it. I have my G.E.D. certificate and I have my real life diploma that I got in 1978. I love it. I show it to everyone that comes in. But I think the thing I'm most proud of is a walnut plaque, copper front panel that says: "Fay Imogene Key, Highest Grade Point Average, Adult High School Completion Class of 1978." So, I thank God for the sight, sound, smell, feel, taste and so forth, but "Thank God" mainly for memory!

142/MY LIFE IN BITS 'N' PIECES

I graduated from Holland High School in 1978.
I was only 57 years old.

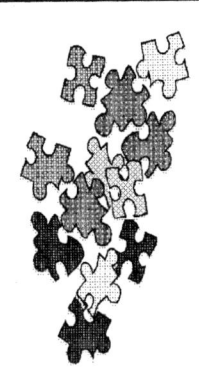

Overly Confident, Sometimes

No one will let me try, but I believe I could actually run this world I live in! The reasons for this belief are many. I'll name some of them. My children think I'm smart. Six out of my seven do. (One does not confirm, does not compute, does not speak to me, does not admit I am her mother!) The other six bring me all kinds of questions and expect an answer. If their friends are about to make, what my children presume to be a serious decision, they will bring them to me. "Mom, tell her/him that won't work. Listen to my mom, she knows." Not to boast, but, I tell them what to do. Sounds simple, don't you think?

Here's another reason. I've been around for seventy-one years, and I know a lot of stuff about stuff. I'm always volunteering advice to people. They usually do what they want to. That gives me room to say, later, "I told you and you wouldn't listen. Next time, you'll listen."

Another reason is I raised seven children by myself. No babysitters, no parents and no welfare. That should speak volumes to modern-day mothers. All of my children are rather well-adjusted adults, if I do say so myself. Six out of seven is a pretty good average.

And if that's not enough to prove I should be able to run the world, I have one last and probably most convincing reason. I graduated, head of my class, at the young age of fifty-seven years. I bet you'd vote for me now, wouldn't you? Well, good!

For you see, I've carried this great load of wisdom and knowledge around under my arm for as long as I can remember. Giving it out at every corner to everyone I meet, whether or not I've been asked.

Why, I've even discussed religion and politics with the best of them, and those are the two bad subjects. And I did a good job, too. Sometimes I've wondered why I didn't convince my opponent I was right. But I was certain he/she would come to their senses, and later admit I was right after all.

But recently I've had some questions of my own, and I don't find answers as readily as I once did. Like, "Why don't the Tigers do better? What in the world is wrong with the Lions? And on whose authority did they trade off the best Pistons on the team?" Earth shaking events!

So now I've failed me! So now I'm seeing myself in a different light. I find that I know nothing save Christ and Him crucified. I know I am no longer my own, but I've been bought with a price. I know there is no condemnation in my life as long as I walk in Him. So, it would seem I've gone from knowing most everything to claiming to know nearly nothing, and I'm still a winner.

As Brother Upthegrove would say, "Ain't that something?" I hope my children aren't disappointed when they find out I don't know as much as they thought I knew.

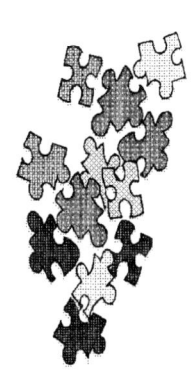

Thank God for Ears

When I awaken each new day and become alert and aware of the fact that I am, I immediately remember I am fearfully and wonderfully made, and I am very grateful to the Maker. And I am so glad I have ears!

In this world of many different sounds, one's ears are constantly bombarded with a multitude of different sounds. Some are harsh, some are soft. Some are high and some are low, and there are sounds of all the varying degrees in between. Some sounds are soothing and some are even painful. Most are gone as quickly as they came and some are indelibly implanted in the mind and soul, and can never be forgotten, even in a lifetime.

One of my earliest memories is of my father's lovely baritone voice singing an old song, "Through the pines, through the pines, where the sun never shines," etc...I could not forget, even if I wanted to. It is permanently engraved in my heart. Like many others, sounds of laughter and cries of sorrow.

I will remember the sound of my mother's sobbing at the funeral of my tiny baby brother. I didn't understand at that time what was happening, but I remember the sound. Never will I forget.

And even now, as I reflect on the past, specific sounds emerge and I remember once more.

I recall vividly the gurgling, tinkling laughter of my firstborn son. It is like a metallic wind chime in my memory. Forever a part of me. I also remember the choking, croupy cough of that same child when he was about three years of age, and he contracted the dreaded disease of diphtheria. I remember vividly the cough.

I remember hearing my first airplane. I also remember the first Cotton Belt Freight Train, up close. The sound was totally terrifying. I thought I would die!

I once concentrated on a single butterfly and felt I heard the faint murmur of its tiny wings. Imagination? I don't think so.

Several times I have heard the screeching of an overprotective mother Blue Jay, standing guard over young ones.

In 1934 we actually heard millions of tiny teeth in thousands of tiny mouths as a hoard of army worms devoured our cotton crop. There was no way to record these sounds, at that time, but they are recorded in my memory for all time.

And then recently I heard the terrifying sound of death! My brother died. And the not breathing was much louder and more paralyzing than the breathing had been. And out of the pain and fog of that awful time, I remember the sound of slow, halting footsteps on the soft, green April grass in a cemetery somewhere.

I remember the inaudible screams that seemed to press upward from the very depth of my being, crisscrossing in my throat until it bled. No one heard except me. And as I looked down on a small piece of marble and read the measure of a man's life in these simple words:

>Billy B. Underwood
>Seaman First Class
>World War II
>Born August 10, 1924
>Died April 7, 1988

a horrendous jumble of sound poured over me like a great river and somehow, in the midst of it all, I recognized the sound of a broken heart.

I remember two more sounds. An anguished voice saying, "Lord, I don't believe I can bear this," and His voice saying softly, "Fear not, for I am with you, even to the end of the world."

And in His voice I heard the infinite sound of love.

Just Another Chapter in My Life

I don't know the reason, but I got up this morning with the feeling that it's time to pen another chapter of my life. There's no great sadness or sorrow to write about, no unusual disturbances (the usual ones are enough, thank you very much), but I just want to write, for the record, so to speak.

I have seven children and I have a very good relationship with six of them. A pretty good average, don't you think? They have all had some struggles in their lives but they all seem very well adjusted now. There have been three divorces out of seven and that always leaves hurt and problems. But for the most part, they have gotten through that phase of their lives. And I've gotten to the place where I can sleep through the night (with no problems or emergencies) and I'm totally at peace with the world, except for one girl. We've had this "thing" for several years. I've done everything I can to fix it, without any success! I do pray! But other than this one situation, I am happy in my life, secure in my salvation and grateful for the joy the Lord has provided for me. Now, for the children.

My oldest son is a great mechanic, and he keeps all my cars in good shape. And, for free! We talk often and have a good understanding between us. My daughter, Star, is a certified gardener and knowing what a large place gardening holds in my life, she keeps me supplied with all kinds of plants. My next daughter, Holly, is a veritable whirlwind. She's always been my fun child. Most always she's the life of any party, or get-together. She's full of fun and jokes and a real joy to be around, most of the time! Ha! The next daughter is Melodi. She lives with me and I lean on her, sometimes heavily. Due to some poor decisions she made in her early adult years, she has had some hard times. But due to the deep pride that I instilled in all of my children, she didn't lay around crying about bad luck and hard times. She's worked all of her adult life (since she was sixteen years old) and supported herself and her two boys with practically no help from their father. She is now engaged to a good man who treats her real well and accepts her two boys, also. So things are going well for her now. My youngest daughter, Quaita is married with two children and seems to be doing well. But I look at her sometimes and think I see a deep down sadness I don't understand. Now, it's okay if she doesn't want to confide everything in her life with me. It just tells me she is being responsible and taking care of herself in the best way possible. And too, I may be letting my motherly instinct get in the way of my better judgement! Everything is probably fine. I surely do hope so. And now I'll get to the reason for this latest episode in the continuing saga of me and mine.

My third child, a son, Billy-Jon is the subject of this chapter. Now, don't tell anyone that I said this, but he's always been so special and I don't know why. In the 70's he had some drug problems. In the 80's he got a divorce and was left to raise his two children alone with practically no help from their mother. Maybe this is where the pity comes in. Now I know many women have been left to raise their children alone, but it's not often a man's fate. I've raised my seven alone after the youngest one was six months old, so I know it can be done. And now, I'm not talking about welfare, but talking about a job. Thanks to General Electric Company here in Holland I was able to take care of my family quite well.

But once they were grown and married I could no longer take care of them. But back to Billy. I guess it's not possible to share as much with a boy as you can with another female child, but I've always felt I was standing ready to pick him up in case he fell. I've only been able to help him a little when the kids were small. But he has basically stood on his own feet and taken care of his business alone. Now the kids are sixteen and nineteen years old, and it seems they don't need either one of us much anymore. So recently he's come up with what I think is a great idea, where he and I can have some quality time together. He now comes over nearly every Saturday morning and takes me out to breakfast. In this way we have time to catch up on what's happening in his life and mine. I just love the time spent together. I don't want to ever be a bother to him or a clinging vine. I just want to enjoy him from time to time.

I sum this up by saying, except for my one great heartache, my life is full, my joy complete. I am a happy and well-adjusted mother! Right here I thank God for His faithfulness in bringing me from where I was to where I am. But that's another chapter.

My future seems clear and bright. I trust God to complete the good work He began in me way back in 1942.

I've climbed some high hills and coasted through some valleys but wherever I am, at any certain time, you be assured I'm having a great time. And as Forrest Gump would say, "That's all I've got to say about that."

Billy and his daughter, Teah

155/MY LIFE IN BITS 'N' PIECES

Billy and a friend, Ann Miley

The Night I Was Saved

This was in July or August of 1943, I think! I lived in Arkansas, right in the center of the best cotton growing country in the world. I'm not talking about growing more cotton than any other place in the world, but more cotton per acre. And that's a documented fact. And that still did not make it a good place to live!

I had married a stranger in February 1940. I guess I wanted to get away from home, but he was so much stranger that by February of 1943 I was back at home. My reason for going back? Well, not all women look good in black eyes and fat lips. I looked especially bad, so I went home. Now I'm back where it all started.

This year, like every other year I could recall, my dad plowed the land, planted the cotton and we all hoed the cotton when it came up and was big enough that we could distinguish it from the weeds. Dad continued to cultivate and we continued to hoe the crop until the plants began to blossom. By then it was too big to work in so we quit working in the fields and just let it grow to maturity. This was about the first of July. Then we got to loll around till the first week in September. Then we started to pick the crop or harvest it. Here was pay for all the hard work we had done. But we were very glad for the two months we had to just do as we pleased, for the temperature got up to 90 degrees real early in the day and didn't bother to cool off till late bedtime. Now this was in the time before TVs and a lot of other forms of entertainment, so we lived a very dull life when we weren't in the field.

About this time a young Pentecostal preacher came through the country, looking for a place to begin a revival meeting. In this neighborhood there was an empty, one-room schoolhouse. I don't think anyone really wanted him preaching there, but no one cared enough to stop him, so the revival began. And just for a cure from the boredom, we all went.

I didn't go to hear what he had to say, I knew it would all be wrong. Had my mother not told me, if it wasn't Baptist it wasn't worth listening to. But there I sat, night after night, giggling and playing silly games, talking and disturbing everyone near me. I was a very sinful sinner at that time!

Looking back with my 20/20 vision, I can see something starting to take hold of me. Not suddenly, but rather subtly. I was hearing things, and they were staying in my mind. I kept thinking of one sermon where he preached about fighting with beasts at Ephesus. I didn't know it was the Apostle Paul's teaching I Corinthians 15:32. I didn't know who this person was, but it got to me. "This is not fair", I thought.

If I had known what was happening, I probably wouldn't have gone back. But isn't it wonderful how the Holy Spirit knows how to set the hook and get ready for the reeling in?

I well remember, 55 years ago now, sliding down the bench I was sitting on until I got to the outside edge. I stepped over the framework that held the benches together and started (very slowly) down toward the pulpit where the young man was preaching. I was not totally aware of what was happening but I went on anyway. It was not by any desire or effort of mine, just a gentle pulling or drawing of the Holy Spirit. There was no feeling of putting my feet in front of the other, I just went! And when I came up even with the front row of people, I remember a feeling of near panic. "Oh Lord," I thought, "everybody's going to see me." So I went to the lady on the front row, Josie White, and I asked her if she would go to the altar with me. Of course, she did and the rest is history, I guess. I don't remember ever hearing you had to quit smoking when you became a Christian, but I knew full well, that I could not smoke another cigarette. And I didn't!

Did God deliver me from the nicotine habit? No! I just knew it was over. Settled! Was it hard? Yes. Did I pray a lot and cry some? Yes. But I never did smoke again. I don't remember when I stopped wanting a cigarette, but I did stop. I guess God saw my determination and helped me a little!

P.S. There's one thing here I think you northern friends may need to know. Did you ever hear about a brush arbor? This was nearly a brush arbor. It was really hot at this particular time. After about four days in the schoolhouse we had to move it outside. So here's what we did. The men laid flat boards on blocks of wood. Then they hung a long string of naked light bulbs in the trees and we had church. I'm so glad we did! It was cool out there. People weren't so hard to please then!

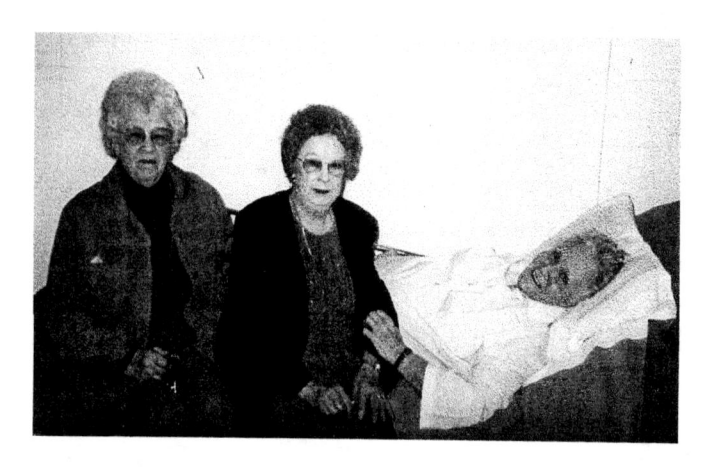

Sally Hobbs, Josie White (the woman who walked to the altar with me 57 years ago), and me

They Are Not All Bad

I had an experience on June 12, 1996 that I need to share. I'll go around the world probably before I'm through sharing, and for that I apologize. But that's just the way I am.

I have a daughter and her two sons living with me. One boy is nine, not too bad. The other one is twelve going on twenty. He gets more phone calls in a day than I get in three months. I get so frustrated with this. Sometimes I get really "ugly" when I answer the phone. I class all kids in a group. And I know that's not really fair, but I just DO. And now.

I was sitting in my window last Wednesday, writing, when two strange girls came up to my door and knocked. I almost insulted them at first, because I figured it was someone looking for the twenty-year-old who is twelve. But for some reason I went to the door and greeted them properly. I am so glad I did. I found them wise beyond their years. I guess they were about fourteen or fifteen years old.

The first thing they did was compliment me on my yard and flowers. A wise choice of words! They must have guessed I was a great lover of gardening and flowers. So I started taking them from one flower to another, telling them what it was, where it came from, who gave it to me and other important things about it. They seemed to enjoy the tour. I know I did! So as we talked we got onto Christianity and just had the greatest fellowship.

After we had visited for a while, and they were getting ready to leave, they asked me if there was anything they could pray with me about. I was a little surprised but so very excited. I told them of my dream of getting a book published. I write poems and short stories. So they agreed with me to this end. There we stood in the daylight, in the middle of the flower garden, me in my duster and nightgown. We held hands and asked God to make me able to get a book published. Imagine that from teenagers!

The girls each prayed aloud and in their turn they thanked God for letting them meet me. I was so blessed. They made me feel like I was a real person, like I was appreciated. A great feeling since most young people don't want to be around the elderly for different reasons. They don't know how to communicate or they are afraid they won't be understood or accepted as real people. Some just don't have time for old folk!

Well, I know they made my heart glad, and I believe God was pleased with their witness and testimony. Now for the big question. Why do the BAD kids get all the newspaper and TV time? Let's give our good kids a break! Thanks girls, you surely made my day.

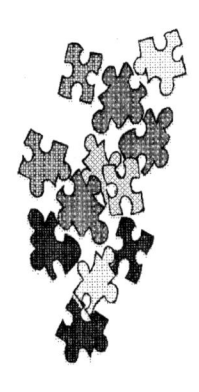

I Have a Question

But first, let me state my reasons for all the questions. I've been noticing quite a few changes lately. At first I did not think too much about it, but lately I've become concerned.

It seems to be a lot further from my house to the store than it used to be. And I haven't moved!

It takes me a lot longer to walk around the block, and the block hasn't gotten any longer!

My flight of stairs is much steeper than when I moved here, thirty years ago.

The newly-cut grass grows back much faster than it once did.

The neighbor's kids are a lot rowdier and much louder than mine ever were.

The food I used to love does not seem as tasty as it once did.

Birthdays and Christmases seem closer together than when I was a kid. Much closer!

The sun seems hotter and the winter wind much colder now. I don't understand!

Even the soil in my garden is harder to till, and grass and weeds are much healthier and more stubborn and determined.

There have been many changes in my life, and I don't refer to puberty and menopause. I'm really getting concerned. So if there is a logical reason for any or all of these changes, I need to know what it is.

Can someone help me, please?

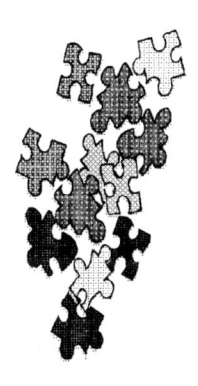

The Importance of Time

I think you've all heard the expression, "God has a sense of humor," and it just may be true. One thing I know for sure, He picks the most unexpected ways to teach us a truth.

Recently I found myself learning a lesson I thought I already knew. It came from a simple job most people think nothing of, but with me it was different. I had been needing a new carpet for a very long time. So when my children gave me a sizeable amount of money for my birthday, I decided to add the rest and get this long awaited carpet. Sounds simple, don't it? But not so. We're not talking about hiring experienced people to do this job. I'm talking about doing this job the old-fashioned way, meaning me and whoever wants to help me.

Now I jump ahead of my story to the bottom line. It looks great! I'm very happy with the outcome. What more is there to be said? But you, knowing me, can be sure I have more to say.

On August 3 I decided to start the job. So I began to clean drawers, clear out the china cabinet, empty the buffet, move everything out of the entertainment center, clear out a large desk full to overflowing with outdated Artex and Tri-chem paints and supplies, and this was just for starters.

Have you any idea how much "stuff" a person can collect in thirty years? So I began. And finding a place to store all the "stuff" was another job. My kitchen was full. My bedroom was full. I just had a tiny path from the door to my bed, and by stretching, I could reach the clothes closet. Things were put in the basement and upstairs. I even put a bunch of potted plants on the patio or outside. I had growing plants coming out of the breadbox and heading for the blender. It was real scary, especially at night. Little furry prickery, hairy things would reach out for me—on my way to the bathroom.

After all of this, we began to rip up the old carpet and take it outside. Then came the many hours of scraping, sweeping and breathing black dust. Just to go to bed, beaten, and get up the next day and scrape and sweep and pick up the filth and breathe more black dust.

Finally on August 13, the professionals came and put the new carpet down. Thank the Lord! Job done—or is it? No, it's not even half done. I have nothing to sit on, and I do dearly love to sit. There's no TV, and that's a big part of everybody's life. I'm no exception!

So begins the job of finding all my "stuff." My daughters and one son-in-law finally get the heavy things back in place, and I start to replace the "stuff." Box after box of glass trinkets, all the things that are trash to others, but treasures to me. And each and every one of them has to be washed. I knew my house was old and dusty, but this is ridiculous. I washed the top edges of every picture on the wall. I took down the curtains, washed them and hung them on the line, and then returned them to their place. There was nothing left untouched. I cleaned everything!

Big deal, you may say! Don't most people clean their houses on a regular basis? Well, you have to understand something. I've had two shoulder surgeries in the last six or seven years. My daughter has lived in my house and did most of the cooking and housework, so this was the first time in many years that I've thoroughly cleaned my whole house by myself. It was a big and time-consuming job. And now the living room and bedrooms are finished, and I'm glad. Still gotta' do the kitchen.

And now, I'll bet you're wondering, "Where is the lesson learned about time," aren't you? Well, here it is. Had the Lord chosen this particular time to return for His bride, I might have been awfully busy with the things of this life that I felt were needful and long overdue. So while I was busy cleaning my house in preparation for a new rug, I was reminded of another housecleaning that we all have to be mindful of. Our spiritual house. We must never let it get spotted with the things of this life. We must not allow things of this dirty world to creep in and soil our spiritual house. We must be doubly alert to the dust and grime of everyday living that will try to get inside and spoil our inner sanctuary that we must keep clean for the Master. There is no time to get careless about our lives. We must get ready and stay ready.

And everything around us, TV, newspapers, news articles, things on every hand, neighbors, and even people in church are saying, "Loosen up a bit. Why are you so serious? God doesn't mind if you have a little fun. What's wrong with a movie once in a while? Does

God really mind if you smoke? Or have a small drink once in a while?"

I feel we should rid ourselves of every weight and sin that could be the cause of our stumbling, and run the race before us with all diligence. This is not the time to be letting down our guard. If the good man had known at what time the robber would be at his house, he would not have been asleep. It's no time for Christians to be careless.

I feel it is time to be alert and ready!

A Trip to South Dakota

I have just returned from a trip to South Dakota. What an experience! I will try to describe some of the country between here and there. And as I had never been in that part of the United States, it was all new and beautiful beyond words, exciting and wonderful to me. I've traveled Rt. 80 through Chicago, going west to Rt. 57. We usually turn south here to go to Arkansas. But we traveled 90 all the way up and through Wisconsin to LaCross, and there we turned straight west, crossing the muddy Mississippi River into Minnesota.

And here the land began to change. We saw more cornfields, silos, more cattle and some houses in the distance. It was all very beautiful, but very different from my home state. I remember we passed near Rochester, Albert Lea, Fairmont and Worthington. You don't see much from the freeway, except the freeway.

We spent the night in Sioux Falls, South Dakota, and immediately the land began to change. No more silos, no cornfields, just rolling ground swells with hayfields and hay bales! Some fields were freshly cut leaving brown stubble, but other fields were every shade of green from light to dark. Some fields were a pale purple where the vegetation was in bloom. I think this was vetch. Everywhere there were hay bales, hay bales. In fact, there was no way the bales could be counted, if you had the time or the inclination to try. And always and forever the prairie stretched away as far as one could see. A wonderful sight this prairie, always changing, yet always the same! And if the sun, wind and rain, or the lack thereof, hasn't changed it in all these centuries, I'm sure I'll never live to see it change.

Somewhere near Dacoma, Minnesota we crossed the wide Missouri River. What a totally awesome sight! It literally brought tears to my eyes. And, not to compare God with part of His creation, but it felt like a religious experience. I trembled. I wept. It was like when you are under a strong anointing from God. I was so aware of God as the creator. I thought of King David's feelings of awe when he viewed God's greatness and asked, "What is man that Thou art mindful of him?" It was a grand sight for my eyes.

The time passed and the miles flew by and, as we neared the western end of the state, we also neared our destination, Rapid City, South Dakota. For several miles we had been getting little glimpses of the Badlands and the Black Hills, which is something I'd advise everyone to try to see in this life. Rapid City is a very beautiful place, and it's not too small either! It's home to about 55,000 people. There are two small towns, on either side, and they are about to merge. Also Ellsworth Airforce Base is near. They are about to come together and form a nice city of 84,000 folk.

But I didn't travel to South Dakota just to see the lay of the land. Ever since I first heard of the monument to Crazy Horse, I've wanted to see it, Crazy Horse having been one of my greatest heroes of all time. I have lots of heroes, all of them being Indians. There's Cochise of the Apache, Osceola of the Seminole, Chief Joseph of the Nez Perce, Quanna Parker of the Comanche, Roman Nose, Black Kettle, Sitting Bull, Red Cloud and Geronimo. Shall I continue?

I went to Rapid City to attend the W.C.G.I.P. That means "World Christian Gathering of Indigenous People." It was co-chaired by Terry LeBlanc and Richard Twiss.

Because of the work schedules of my people, we couldn't leave until Thursday morning. My granddaughter drove all the way. We spent the night in Sioux Falls, South Dakota and got to Rapid City about noon the next day. All the way my negative talking daughter-in-law had her doubts and fears about which she was very verbal. I kept telling them God would work it all out.

At one time a red light came on in the car. It was a new car, so there was no reason for a light to come on. And I admit it was a reason for a bit of concern for a moment. So we put our heads together, we three women and the four-year-old boy, and made a decision. We knew how to start the car, stop the car, put gas in the car, and that was about all! But through it all I felt at peace about it. I was not afraid, for I had bathed the trip in prayer for weeks before we left home. I had even asked God to send angels to comfort, guide and protect us, so I didn't feel any great fear. I told my family often that God would work it all out and, by the time we got home, Kathy was telling her husband, "She told us it would be okay," just like it had been her idea all along.

And now we're off to see Mt. Rushmore! What a marvelous thing to see! What a price they charge for their trinkets! But I did enjoy every minute of it.

My daughter-in-law, Kathy,
my granddaughter, Terry,
and my great-grandson, Nick,
in front of Mt. Rushmore

Still, all the time we spent paying our respects to Abe, George, Teddy and Thomas, I was really anxious to get on over to THE monument—The Crazy Horse Monument! It was fifteen miles further down the road. I had this feeling of awe as we approached this greatest of all carvings. A whole mountain. When I raised my head and had my first look at the one reason I was in South Dakota, it took my breath away.

I don't know if I'm reading more into this than I ought, but I could actually feel the spirit of the warrior who gave everything he had to keep his people free, hovering over the Black Hills, his Paha Sapa (place where the great spirit dwells). I felt a great joy just to be there but, at the same time, an achy sadness for all he and his people suffered at the hands of us. And I've been weeping ever since for the sins of my people. I awaken in the night and cry for this gigantic injustice that was perpetrated on a people who had not sinned against us in any way at that time! I've asked God many times if there's any way I can help change any of this. Let me say here that I have no special orders, yet.

As I stood there I began to enumerate the wrongs committed. First, all the beaver fur was taken. Then the buffalo hides harvested and the meat left to rot away. The theft of all the silver and gold. The causeless deaths of thousands of people, not just the warriors, but babies, youth and the aged ones. But I think the worst thing was the desecration of their sacred PaHa SaPa (place where the great spirit dwells). What else could have been done?

Earlier I spoke of the spirit of Crazy Horse brooding over the hills, and it was a reality to me. I also heard the long ago cries of the women as they gathered their children close, as they hid them in rocky canyons or as they climbed steep cliffs trying to get away from the soldiers.

All of these cries still whisper to you in the spruce trees. You can hear it in the tall grass as the wind sighs through it. All of this you can hear as you stand quietly and think of the past. I look at my skin and am ashamed of who I am. We all had a part in this.

My great-grandson, Nick, and me
by The Crazy Horse Monument

The Bad Lands in South Dakota

Buffalo in South Dakota

Then on the last day of my visit, I went to the last service of the W.C.G.I.P. I am so glad God has a plan for everything and everybody. All of my life I've wondered how God planned to reach the Indians with the Gospel, and many other nations that have seemingly been overlooked in the broader missionary scheme of things. Well, I still don't know how, but I know He did it. For I worshipped with a large crowd of Indians that Sunday, and I'll never forget it as long as I live.

In church Sunday I heard another cry, but it had a different sound. These Indians were singing a song of praise to a God who had never for one moment forgotten them. They sang of salvation and forgiveness. One sister prayed, "God, forgive us for the many unholy tears we've shed, not knowing that your wounds should have cleansed our wounded hearts." I was so overcome with emotion I just stood and wept.

Some things are good to know. This was one of them!

In Training

This is about my desire to talk about a fight I'm in. Now right away someone's going to say, "This elderly lady doesn't look like a trouble-maker." But I say, "Don't form opinions too quickly, I might surprise you." I wasn't a fighter when I was young. My older sister was everything I ever wanted to be. I adored her! We didn't fight. My younger brother was put here for me to love, so we didn't fight! So how did I get to be such a scrapper you may ask, and that's my story.

I had not been saved very long until I realized I was in a battle. Mostly with myself. Satan bringing all of my earthly ugliness up to become my enemy. The first battle was with cigarettes. I was a smoker! So I fought and cried and prayed a lot. We were not taught that God would deliver us from the nicotine habit. He didn't give me the habit, so I didn't ask him to take it away. I figured it was my problem and responsibility to get rid of it. I never smoked again after I went to the altar to be saved. It was a battle and somehow, without understanding spiritual things, we won!

Then there was the battle over words. I had always been used to a lot of slangy talk. Not horrendous swearing, just careless slang, and I found myself slipping in this area many times. Not out of anger, just habit. So I cried again many times and prayed over this. I would love to say it was like the first battle, but not so. Until this very day, I have to be on guard when I repeat a story, for I tend to repeat verbatim. I need to be accurate, I say.

Those two battles were specific. There have been many others. Most of them, I won. Some of them, I didn't. Through it all I've fought with all of my might.

But recently, in 1998, I think I've been fighting the greatest battle of my life, and it's been far worse than whether I'd pick up a cigarette and light it or not. A cigarette is such a small little enemy!

This recent and far greater battle has been about my daughter, Melodi, who had cancer surgery on March 30, 1998. After that seemed to be getting better, she had a cyst on the one remaining fallopian tube that had to be removed. Now she has an infection in the same area, giving us yet more trouble.

And though I've never been too far from the front lines of battle, and I thought I could stand anything, this year has taken its toll on me. I've spent nights with my troubled thoughts, and I've walked through my days in tears and prayers—again! This has been the apex of all my fighting, for it's been so very close to my heart. I call this enemy FEAR!

Now I know I'm supposed to be a woman of faith, and yes, I do believe God's word. But I'm also a mother. This one has been a BIG one. I've been very tired at times. It's been a struggle. I've known extreme weariness in my body and in my spirit. I remember King David praying for the wings of a dove that he might fly away and be at peace. I've known that feeling. But I know also, that I can't quit now.

I signed up for the duration way back in 1943. Nothing was said about the end of the war. He said, "Occupy until I come," and I haven't seen Him anywhere yet, have you? So I fight on.

Written December 2, 1998

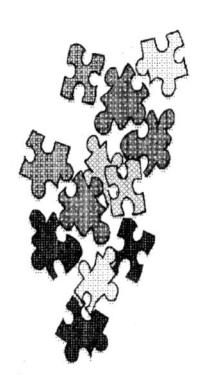

The Posture of Pain

Imagine the pain as all invasive, excruciating, life consuming, and it is by no means all physical. The mind screams itself into a state of numbness, alternating between hope and total despair.

There is not enough air to maintain life. The arms stretch upward in an effort to make room for more air in the lungs, but as the arms reach up and more space is made, the pain grows and fills the accommodating space.

The body convulses and bows down to expel the air and pain, very much like the contractions of a woman in the throes of childbirth. Will anything alleviate this pain? Even for just a moment?

We know that if asked, God will send His comfort, but right now it can't be felt. We know His comfort is ours, we know He sent it, but we are unable to feel it. This is such a personal thing! We each have to learn how to deal with our own grief in our own way. And we wonder if it will ever end.

I am no stranger to this kind of pain. I felt it at my parents' death. I felt it especially at my brother's death, and I am feeling it again today over the dead children and their parents and friends in Colorado.

It would sound like the greatest foolishness to say to those living people today, "The God of peace will comfort you."

We know that time will ease the pain, but never erase it completely. In years to come we might find ourselves back in that posture of pain again, asking, "Why?" and over a totally different kind of pain.

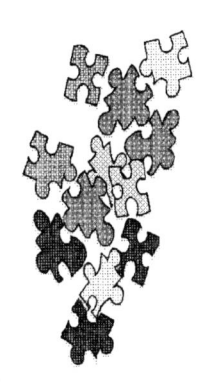

One Large Regret

I'm going to write this in the form of a letter. Maybe I'll be able to say all the things I never was brave enough to say to my mom. Now it is twenty-three years too late to say it to her in person, but anyway—

Dear Mom,

I wish I had been able to talk to you about the really hard or important things in my life as I was growing up, but I could not. You never made it easy. No, I'm not blaming you for my inadequacies, even though you were a part of what I was and what I became and who I am today. I'm a firm believer that we are the product of our environment.

I was a product and so were you. I remember the story of your mother, who died very young of tuberculosis when you were only eight years old. After living for a year with an older half-sister, you went back home to keep house for your father, get meals for two younger siblings, get the three of you off to school, and do all the things a mother would have done. I know you washed clothes on a scrub board, hung them on a line to dry, and later you had to iron them with an iron that was heated on a wood stove. I also remember the stories of your upbringing. How your father, being of the Quaker persuasion, did not believe in wasting anything. He allowed you to bake a cake, but you couldn't put frosting on it. It wasn't necessary. It was just one little quirk, among others, in his nature.

I know you wanted more out of life than my father provided for you. It was just one more disappointment in a life filled with many more. Even the times were against you. You and Dad were married in 1916, with WWI before you and the entire Great Depression thrown in for good measure.

As I look back I cannot see one good day, financially, in your lives. To say that your first security came with advancing age would not be an exaggeration. I know my life was one step better than yours, and that, too, was dictated by the times. We faced WWII, but there were more jobs, more money and a different place for women in the world, thanks to gals like Rosie and Riviter. There was a general upgrade in the way we lived.

My father never seemed to feel too badly about the lack in our lives. I'm sure he cared, but not the way you cared. I think that is one of the major differences in Moms and Dads. But through it all he was a jolly, carefree, happy (?) man. He was so easy to love! But you were so loaded with cares and concerns about the family, you never seemed happy. I know now, in part, how you felt. I saw my children's needs for things and I blamed their father. Who else could I blame?

I used to wonder why you were always so angry, or unhappy or sad. Now I know. I wish I could have known sooner. I wish I could have said, "Mom, it's okay to be disappointed in life. It's okay to expect more than you ever have a hope of getting. I do understand, Mom, really I do." I wish I could have said a lot of things like, I loved you in spite of your being unapproachable. I wish I could have said it, but I never did.

I AM SO SORRY!

Sincerely,
Gene Key

A Journey—Oases in My Desert

This morning as I was in prayer with no plan or intent on my part, I found myself remembering and praying for people who had been a great blessing to me at different times in my life. Some people from faraway, in terms of years, and some more recently, like in the year of 1999. And my next thought was, I've got to write this down. It might serve as a reminder to someone else that we didn't get to where we are all by ourselves!

First, we had to come to Christ. Perhaps someone told us or explained the way to us. Now some may say, "Oh, I was born and raised in a Christian home." And I say, "Big deal. That don't make you a Christian." God's word says, "Ye must be born again." Okay? So now we're saved, what's next? Well, the road of life is straight ahead, and it doesn't always go through the flatlands of Arkansas. Sometimes the road takes us through and over the Rocky Mountains of the West! Sometimes we find ourselves in the low, wet, boggy delta of Louisiana. At times we may get mired down with the load we carry, or we might fall off a mountain in our climb, if we are left to our own devices.

So if I know this now, God surely knew it then and made provisions for just such times in our lives. So He, in His great omnipotence, put people along the way who would come to our aid when we were weary of the way, when our strength was almost gone. I think of all of them as God's glue that held my frail barge together in many a storm! This may be my way of trying to thank them all. So from the beginning—

I was saved in 1943. I was from a family that didn't know and never used the word "saved." I heard of joining the church, or turning over a new leaf, or getting a letter of transference when you moved. But saved? That we will see about in time.

So I started on my journey! It began in 1943 and it was a struggle, for I never found my first oasis until I moved to California in 1948. It was there I found a great church and my pastor taught me how to lean on God and His word and His understanding. I had spent five years hanging onto my salvation by the skin of my teeth and what little I knew about the Bible. And what I did know was head knowledge, not spirit! But I did begin to put down roots. And still today I thank God for His written word and His well-placed oasis along the way.

I had married in 1945, and I soon knew I had made a very large boo boo! I had missed God's plan for me, but knowing divorce was not an option I tried to do the best I could and not complain. Knowing I had made a poor choice, I was still determined to make the best of it. So began a long road, many hurtful things and many children. The children made all the other pain bearable, worthwhile! They were my only joy.

I went to whatever church I was near. I was fed just barely enough to keep hanging on. My husband was not a Christian, so he did not get up every Sunday wondering how he could get his wife and her children to church.

Then in 1951 we moved to Michigan. I found a good church, made many friends who would go out of their way to take us to church. Another oasis.

Then sometime later I started on a trip that would lead into a wilderness situation beyond belief. But while I floundered, for several more years, I still had God's provision for my life. And I now call them God's oases from heaven: the water of love in a parched and dry land.

I don't know why He loved me so much. I sometimes wonder why He did not cut me loose and let me go. But that's not His way. He is longsuffering! And He kept placing safety zones in the way, where He knew I'd need them most.

So, right now, in 1999, I finally feel safe. And it was not anything I did, but His plan and purpose is finally falling into place. I can feel the solid ground beneath my feet, at last. And I'm grateful in a way that most of you could never understand. It's about time!

And another thing: if you ever feel like giving a compliment to anyone or a word of encouragement, please do it with all haste before your brain tells you, "Maybe this is not a good time." It's always a good time. And it just might be the very time someone needs help getting over a huge mountain. Someone may be in a battle of a lifetime and asking God to send help. There may be a friend ready to sink in a slough of despondency, and your words of encouragement can have far-reaching effects. Be an oasis! Don't be stingy with the gifts God has given you.

And now, as I struggle with the last part of my story, I don't know if it's all right to name names or not, but the Apostle Paul did. But there are so many who have helped me along the way—I'm not at all sure I can remember all of them. So I'll just say, "Thank you, Father, for Pastor Simms in California. And for Pastor Simmons in South Haven, Michigan. And thanks for Pastor Fred and Pastor Randy here in Holland.

Thank God for all the oases I've found in my times of need.

More About Oases

I think most of these things began after the death of my husband. So I call this the desert of my discontent!

I was actually glad when he left us, but I never could have believed what a double hardship it left us in. I had always made all of the decisions for the children and me, as far as going to church. There wasn't much else I could make decisions about, for we didn't always have a car or gas. And you can't walk far when you are pregnant or have three, four, five, or more children to take along. I had no phone or no money, so we stayed at home when the kids were not in school.

After my husband had been gone a year and a half, he was killed in a car wreck of his own making. Drunk and running! A brother from our church in South Haven took the kids and me to Arkansas to his funeral. By now the oldest boy and girl were in jail and couldn't attend their dad's funeral.

And after the reality of all this sank in, I came home under the heaviest load a person can walk with. Later, when I looked back, still looking for the culprit I could blame, this seemed to be it. Overburdened with life's toils. If this was not the reason, I still do not know what was.

Then I entered a phase of life I called the desert of my own confusion, in which I was searching for something I could hold onto and trust in. Not realizing I was slowly letting go of the only bit of stability in my life. I questioned everything. I said, "I didn't ask for this situation. I was a good mother and wife. I did the best I could with what I had to do with. This is not fair." And later, I was to remember the nights my husband came home at three or four a.m., after his night out on the town, and occasionally he would reach for me, and I would freeze or turn away from him. A very human thing to do, but was it a Christian thing to do? I still do not know!

And then came a time of stumbling. Do you know what follows stumbling? You fall! Then my unsettled and unsure lifestyle brought me to a time of waywardness. And from waywardness it was one step to sinfulness.

So my time of sin, which is still hard for me to face and acknowledge without extreme shame and pain, began. And I say here, oh, but for the gentle grace of God!

But, as I now in 1999, look back I can recognize and be thankful for all the people that were situated in just the right places when I so fearfully needed them. I think of them as the water of God's love in my desert land. I probably can't place them in exactly the right time in my life. But, if they read this, they will know how very much I love and appreciate them. Forgive me if I forget someone.

There was Josie White, who walked with me to the altar in 1943. Thanks to Sally Hobbs, who brought us together in 1999, after fifty-six years!

In South Haven there was Sister Butler, Margaret Appenzellar, Grace Hiatt, and Vareta Couey-Chase, who attended to our many needs from '52 till '69. Grace continued to see after us until her death in 1999.

Then there is Ann Hart, Shar Koenig and Flavia Crowner. They all know how much they have helped me.

And when I need to lean on someone, even now, I could never forget Agnes French, Edna Wenger and Laura Greathouse. Jean Shaw is very special also. She shares with me her ministry.

And then there are three more people, who have been a steadying factor of large proportions in my life, and they were not even Christians. Olga Morgan, Larry Kelch and Mary Nolan. When church people were so disgusted with the way my life had turned, there were still people in my life who could and would help me. This was when I was in my time of utter failure and heartbreak.

To all these people I give my deepest thanks and gratitude. I love all of you much!

They were my oases.

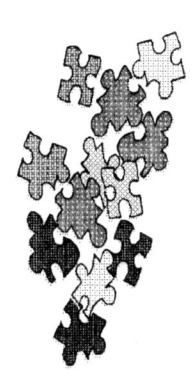

Unruly Thoughts and Things

There are thoughts and things within my heart
That I choose not to speak of.
But they are an integral part of me,
Nevertheless!

For the most part they remain hidden,
Deep within my soul,
Already forgiven by my Lord,
Part of my past, almost forgotten.

But sometimes, like shadows that sneak
Subtly out and about in the even' time,
These ghost-like apparitions begin to appear
To me, and I realize I must again
Exercise my own past.

If it were a danger from without,
I could be in charge of the situation better.
But this thing comes from within me,
Making it more difficult to deal with.

For the most part, this ghost remains quiet,
And in submission to a power, not my own.
But occasionally, whether through a dream,
Or a face in a crowd that reminds me of the past,
Or maybe just a faint little breeze, I "remember,"
And I know I have a fight on my hands.

But since I refuse to be torn between then and now,
I know that I must speak, orally,
To my own ghostly memory,
And with authority, I hope!

And I speak thusly,
"Please leave me in peace.
You have no place in my life now,
So please go away!"

And somewhere deep inside me,
A tiny voice whispers,
"But not too far!"

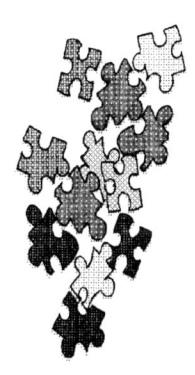

A Place Where I Long to Go

There is a height where a human spirit can go,
If that desire and yearning be there.
A height where many will never go.

There are places where foolish persons have asked
To be allowed to go,
Where only angels dare to walk.
And they know they must tread very softly.

We do so aspire to greatness.
But who will persevere?
Who can stand the test?
Who will scale the heights?

How many will start on this journey,
Only to become weary,
Or tired and discouraged,
Or decide it would be easier,
Just to go with the flow?
These will never know
What they almost had in their hands.

But there are others, who will not be denied.
They know where they want to go and,
Are willing to pay the price to get there,
To that place where the spirit longs to be.

There is an unexplained drawing that will not cease,
Will not be satisfied on any other plain,
Except the very highest.
It's like a pulling of gravity.
The soul of man crying to be free,
To be unrestrained,
To be able to fly.

And when one's determination,
And super-human energy,
Has taken them up and on,
And this highest of crags has been reached,
They find the atmosphere,
Pure, fresh and invigorating.

And there, they find a view that few people
Ever see.
It is a view that cannot be described,
It must be felt.

There is a height where the human spirit can go.

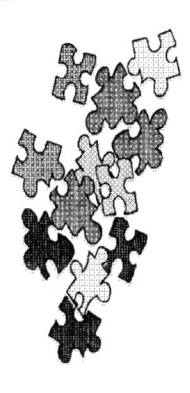

I'll Share

Due to circumstances beyond my control, I've never been able to do a lot of giving, and that's too bad, for I think I'd love it. I know one thing, I've become a great receiver!

God has been so good to me. He has always provided the things I need at the time I need them.

In times past, I remember needing many things that did not appear at the moment. I wondered why my need was being disregarded. I knew God owned the cattle on a thousand hills, so I knew it would not be a problem for Him to get the things to me that I had such need of. I did try hard not to complain, but at times I did wonder! It was much later in life that I came to understand it is not always good to be given everything we want. Check out the spoiled children of today. They are no happier, and certainly no healthier, than those who have less.

And I believe there is a lesson to be learned in waiting. We surely learn patience and appreciation. So, instead of tossing the old toy aside for the new one, we learn to love and appreciate the old. In time we gain a new appreciation for the old and familiar things. And the simple things of life become gifts from the Creator. For instance, the following:

I was walking in my garden (I call it my garden of prayer) a few days ago just after we had had a shower of rain. I was making my usual rounds, inspecting every plant and tree, I do this most every day. I love the blossoms, and I check the progress of everything. I especially look for the new mimosa trees. They appear daily, and I recount them daily. I now have over forty of them from one inch high to some that are adult enough to blossom. Would anyone like to have a mimosa tree of their very own? I'll give you one! I'll share. But, back to the goodness of God in my life.

As I stood under a rose on a trellis, God chose that moment to send a breeze that caused a shower of rain and rose petals to fall on me. Now let me ask you, how many of you have had God greet you in such a manner? I took it as a personal greeting! So I say, "Good morning to you, Lord. I think it's going to be a great day."

Imagine being showered with rose petals! Is that great or what?

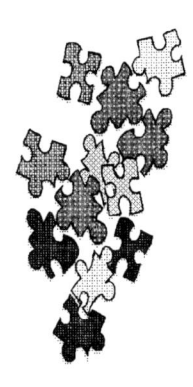

Some Personal Observations

I am a part of God's creation.

I am not anything in and of myself.

I am akin to the sun, the moon, the seasons, the tides and the food crops.

I love God's nature. I know some of my behavior is not acceptable in today's society, but I love the trees, the rocks, the flowers, the soft breezes, even the gales that come in the cold time when most things are asleep!

I talk to my flowers when no one's around. Who, I ask you, but God would remember to make one of every color?

And consider the tropical birds. The colors so brilliant they remind you of a streak of lightning as they pass.

And there are rabbits, coyotes and wolves that are all of earth tones. Not so outstanding in color, but that's all for a purpose, too. Their colors act as a camouflage to let them hide from the hunter. The world is full of predators, man being the greatest one of all. Did you ever hear of an animal killing another animal for the ring on his finger or for the watch he had on his wrist? Did ever an animal kill for a wallet or a car? I think we need to determine here, who is the animal and who is the predator.

And did you ever soar with the eagle or the hawk, even in your imagination? Can you believe a man could shoot an eagle? Why? You can't eat them, so whatever could be the motive for killing this majestic creature? But we know that a man can kill his mother or brother, so why do we think it strange that he would kill an eagle? I believe that when an animal kills, it's for a better reason than that. When a man goes to court for abusing his wife or children, some fine-looking, pinstripe-suited lawyer goes up and shows the judge that this man was abused when he was a child. I guess this is supposed to give him the right to do the same thing to his family.

Does the Bible say anything about, "Do unto others as was done unto you?" Maybe we should bestow a Phd. on a big grizzly and let him teach us about "cause and effect" plus a thing or two about humanity- one to another. Of course, you must know some of this is in jest. But I do have a great desire to see man become what God meant for him to be, not a reasonable facsimile.

And, yes, I do feel a oneness with God in most everything I encounter. The warm sun on my skin. A cool breeze in my face on a hot day. The flutter of a butterfly wing as it darts here and there. I see the awesome face of God in every flower, if I inspect it closely. I am aware of God in the shrill voice of a bluebird or the cantankerous squawk of a crow. He's everywhere and in everything. Yes, some sounds, like some colors, are more pleasant than others, but don't forget their origin. God is the creator of all of them!

And yes, I do love the howling winds that drift the snow around my house in February! It's all a part of who I am. God wrote the story, so I might as well enjoy all of it!

And then, someone wrote a book about the color of Hell! I did not read that!

My Song

There is a song within me that has never yet been sung. It has therefore not been heard. What a shame.

More than once, I've been ready to stand forth and sing, but there's always been a startling interruption to my performance. It's been like the last minute preparation of a grand orchestra tuning up for the final time before the one performance that will place them in musical history as being totally above all others. The feelings are there. Everything is right. The sun and moon are in perfect alignment. It is time for this aria to be sung.

But while preparations are being made, there is a glitch. It's like a violin string broke or the conductor had died. The moment had come and was now gone. The only sound was very much like the sound of a broken heart!

Not a melody. No one sang the song!

I wish I could describe this feeling, but I obviously can't. I cannot write this feeling on a common sheet of paper.

It must be sung!

How can I live and be expected to function with this pain inside of me? Twice in my life I've felt this pain, this need to tell the world, "Look! Hear me! I have something to say! My song needs to be sung."

It may be that I am destined to be like the Thorn Bird, who never sings a song until it impales itself on a thorn and dies with a great song bursting from its throat.

I only hope someone hears me when I sing, and remembers!

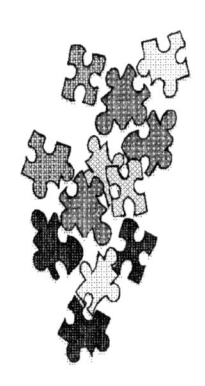

A Lot of Questions

The thing that I most feared is become a part of me. I know I am never alone, so why do I feel lonely? Why does the "clay house" part of me fight so hard with the spirit part of me, the very essence of who I am?

I've told myself often that I despise the clinging, demanding kind of mother who wants her kids to cater to her needs always! And then I find myself thinking, if they needed me, they'd be here. A thought born of selfishness, no doubt.

I know they have homes, families, jobs and obligations of their own. But why does this not fill the empty place in my heart, my need to see, or at least hear, them often? Am I so totally consumed with my needs that I can't be reasonable?

The knowledge in my head does not fill the emptiness in my heart. So the war continues!

Someone might say, "Give your pain to God." And to that I would answer, "I have literally made heavy the ear of God with my crying."

A long time ago, when my kids were small and most of my friends had small kids too, I heard mothers say, "I'll be glad when these kids grow up and learn to do for themselves." Never once did I want mine to get big and go away! I guess I'm kind of weird, wouldn't you say?

Today my house is quiet and empty, and I don't like quiet and empty. Give me noise any day!

After hearing the patter of seven pairs of tiny feet, the quarrels of tots over toys, the arguments of teenagers over whatever, the sounds of a feverish child (four of them at one time) with measles, and the croupy cough of one small boy with diphtheria, how can I ever adjust to a quiet home? It is not natural!

Now that I have exposed my soul or my selfishness, let me hasten to say, "I do want my children to have their own lives, to be happy, to be independent of me."

But I still wonder, why can't we have both?

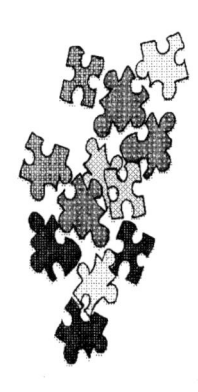

My Aged Aunt's Story

I visited in Arkansas recently with a sister who has Alzheimer's disease. It is a very difficult thing to deal with, and a very sad thing. This sister was a very intelligent person, but is now in a "time warp" somewhere between 1929 and 1936. Her entire life seems to be lived in this era and she only remembers the bad/traumatic things. She repeats them, with venom in her voice, continually, over and over. She tells me I'll soon be just like her, since I'm only two years younger than she. But I know it's not so. I trust God with my life, and I thank Him continually for my sound mind. He gave me this promise in 2 Timothy 1:7, "For God hath not given us the spirit of fear; but of power, and of love, and of a sound mind." I accepted it. And I said all that to say this:

My mind is a marvelous thing. It works overtime. I am always recalling things from my past, from my childhood, and I want to write them down. I want my children to know me by the stories I tell them and maybe understand me better because of them.

Only this morning I remembered a thing that happened many years ago and since I thought it was amusing, I thought I'd write it down. Then it will be placed with my other poems and short stories. I hope to get a book of my thoughts published someday, but they will be here for my kids to read, published or not.

Here is the tale my aged aunt told to me when she was in her 90's. Her mind was very clear also. Her family had come to Flint, Michigan in 1936. They bought a piece of land, saved their money and eventually built their home. You have to understand, my aunt built the house, except for the digging of the basement. She was a carpenter, like all her brothers.

It was a nice home, but she always worried, as she got older, that she had not made the roof steep enough. Something about snow run-off! She began to worry that a very heavy snow would cause the roof to cave in on her some night while she slept. Every time she expressed this thought in my presence, I laughed at her fears. My reasoning being that if it was going to cave in it would already have done it. It was fifty years old. Well, she died a year ago, and she never did get to say, "I told you so."

But she did have cause for alarm a few years ago. A big storm came, a very strong wind storm, and it turned some of her shingles upside-down. They were pointing up instead of down like she had placed them years ago. So when she discovered this, she got her ladder, hammer and tacks and went forth to do battle with nature.

As most folks know, women have not always worn slacks or pants. So up the ladder she went in skirt and blouse, sat herself down on the edge of the roof, and began to tack her shingles back in place, one at a time. In the midst of her labor a neighbor came running around to the back of her house to see what was going on. He came to a shocked stop when he saw this seventy-year-old woman up on the house, and he blurted out, "Mrs. Wilkins, now I've just seen about everything."

To which she answered, "I'll just bet you have!"

Can you imagine that?

To My First Grandchild

I want to begin by saying there has never been a lack of love in my heart for you. But somehow I may have failed to express it as I now feel I should. You are my first grandchild, very special and dearly beloved, maybe even an extension of me. In you, I see my life continuing even after I am no longer here, and that makes me happy.

I wonder why it sometimes takes a tragedy to make us aware of how fragile we actually are. How small a part we play in the "overall" picture of life as God sees it.

I've been looking at you, in the trauma center unit of the hospital, and asking God what I can do to help. I, who am a complete coward where pain is concerned, have been asking God to let me share your pain. I've watched you and the progress has been so very slow, and there have been times when despair would try to take over. But I refuse to accept that. I know in whom I have believed, and I have entrusted your body and your spirit and soul to Him. So I know you are going to get better and better until you are again whole and completely normal.

Remember, Terry, we love you and need you. Mr. Nick, Dan, Kathy, Roy, all of the rest of the family, and I need you!

As you are getting better I seem to see the Lord's arms of love under you, holding you up, caring for you. In my spirit I see His love around you, like a hedge of protection against any outside harm. And I also see above you a canopy of His love covering you. So rest quietly and get well. You are in good hands. He must have a special purpose for your life!

I cannot say all that's in my heart, but please know that I love you! I am anxiously awaiting the day when all your physical pain and your emotional pain will be just a dim memory, and your life will once again be a joy to you and to all of us who love you so very much.

To my first grandchild with love,
GRAMMA KEY

Father's Day

There is a line in a song that reminds me of my father. I don't know who sings it, but it says, "Take a look at these hard-working hands." And since this is June and near Father's Day, I've been thinking a lot of my father. He's been gone since May of 1973, but not many days pass that I'm not reminded of him in one way or another. He was a great singer, and I always find myself thinking-Dad didn't sing that song that way. So I know someone is not singing it right! Even our choir leader doesn't do the songs right. She doesn't know I am comparing her way to the way my dad did it. My dad did know music, so I was not just being picky.

My father grew up without a father from the age of eight. He always had to help his mother in any way he could. When he was twenty, he and my mother were married. They raised five children during The Great Depression. He was a farmer and had to work very hard to feed us. He was a good carpenter also, but there was no money for building houses. So he planted, hoed and picked cotton year after year. Very hard work!

I remember his hands showed the results of all that hard work. I've seen him plow all day for someone else for $.75 a day, not an hour!

I know this would be hard to believe in this modern day and age, but it's true. And you know what? I never heard him complain. There was no way he could change his lot in life, so he quietly accepted it. He was kind and loving, had an upbeat attitude about himself, and just made the best of a bad situation.

We were poor, we didn't celebrate holidays, didn't give gifts or send cards. And I find myself, after twenty years, still wishing I could tell him how much I appreciate what he did for me and how much I loved him and still love him.

A good father is a priceless gift!

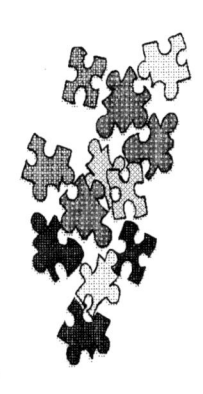

A Glorious Day

Did you ever see a day so absolutely glorious that it made your breath catch in your throat? Did you find yourself wondering, just for a minute, if Heaven could be much better than this?

Today is such a day for me! The colors may be beyond their peak conditions, but I don't miss anything. I've been outside making pictures of all the beauty around me.

At different times in my life I've stood in a warm spring rain that was so delicious, I was mesmerized. I've also gone outside, just for a moment, during a summer downpour, after a long dry spell, and you could smell the earth drinking the rain. You can nearly taste the beauty of it! Or at least, I can.

And don't forget the blizzards of winter that I love so very much, with all the powerful wind and the clean snow that covers a multitude of ugly.

All of these seasons are a joy to my very soul. But today, I believe God decided to outdo Himself! He has been raining gold down on me. Can you believe that?

All shades of gold, floating down, twirling, spinning, tumbling ever so softly. All the time reminding me of a baby's soft kiss, as the gold continues to rain down.

As I breathe deeply and enjoy all the stirring of my senses, I seem to know all is well with my soul. And I am extremely happy!

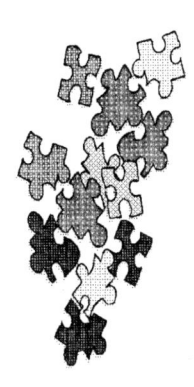

Hints of Despair

I start this story the same way I've started many other stories that concern my family and me. I go way back and start at the beginning.

Recently I had a real battle, not only in the physical, but in the realm of the spirit. My daughter, Melodi, had cancer. Needless to say, it nearly took my breath away. The physical battle was nearly more than I could deal with. The shock of it set me back, so to speak, and a great fear flooded my being like never before. And I began to pray! I soon realized God did not give me a spirit of fear, so I started to work, praying myself through the first steps of the crisis.

One report was fair, the next not so good. Then the next looked better, and the next one took all the wind out of my sails! The doctor said, "Yes, this is cancer. Now here's what we need to do about it." Well, I knew there was nothing I could do, except pray, so I got real serious about prayer. Some time during this intense time of prayer, I was reminded of another scripture. It tells me after I've done all I can-to stand!

So as firmly as I can, with knees knocking loudly, I take my stand. So while I'm standing and praying and begging God for a miracle, or just a healing, or maybe just reasonably good health, I end up just asking that He spare her life! Now I begin to feel a little better about the situation. It's real good to just lean on God and trust Him to do what needs to be done. It's not always easy. I think it's more of a process. It takes time.

So while I'm standing, I begin to go back in my mind to another time and place. I remember the day this child was born! I remember the day my pastor and I dedicated her to the Lord in the church in South Haven. She was always good and dependable. She got herself and her sister off to school when I had to be at work at seven o'clock in the morning. I also remember that she was her father's favorite among the children, though for the life of me, I can't see how a parent can have a favorite. But that didn't stop him from walking away and leaving her and six other siblings and myself sitting along the side of the road. He went back south to live out the rest of his life alone. A poor decision he had to live with.

Some time later, she quit school at sixteen, got a job, bought a car, and started taking care of herself. She paid me a little something for rent. Between the ages of nineteen and twenty-four, she had two children born into a dysfunctional family. This situation was a heart-ache to all of us. But she, being from a dysfunctional family also, just went to work and took care of her family the best way she knew how.

On down the road, she ran into a problem with drugs. This was in the 70's and 80's, and this was a real scary thing. It affected all of us. But in time, the light shown into her darkness. She realized her condition and then began the fight of our lives. Since there was but one way to go, and that's up, she started the long climb.

After she had won the battle with drugs, she found a new job. That's a good start. Eventually there comes a good man, a responsible man, into her life who wants to marry her and take the job of raising her two boys. Now with a commitment between them, they build a new home. Everything is now looking good, but do not count the devil out yet! He is still at work. He does not give up easily. He is still the destroyer of hopes, happiness, health and life!

So now we are back to the beginning. Back to the cancer. Now we have had the surgery, we're getting ready for radiation, and we still have great hopes for the future. And in the midst of all of this, I've seen answered prayer, I've felt His presence, and I still know in whom I have believed. Without the scriptures and His promises, I would have known some unbearable dark nights. So I've turned it all over to Him. Who else is there to go to? Jesus has the power of life and death in His hands. I'm looking forward to the next chapter in this continuing saga!

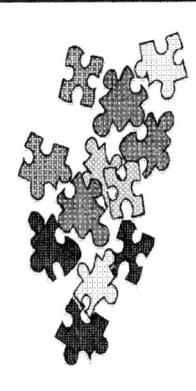

The Uninvited Guest

Recently, the granddaughter of a friend of mine said "My, you have a lot of stories to tell," to which I replied, "Well, if you are 74 years old and have no stories to relate, you are probably already dead and no one has bothered to tell you so!"

So begins this latest one!

About a month ago I awakened with a very sore lump in my neck. Now since every one of my relatives on my father's side of the family has died of cancer, well, a lump is an attention-getter, if you get what I mean. But let me hasten to say that I am in, and have lived in, wonderful health for nearly every day of my life. It's been such a blessing and I'm so grateful for it.

And then with no warning, I have a lump! Now, I'm not afraid, but then why do my fingers continually reach for the lump to see if it is still there or if it is bigger than it was yesterday? And why is it still sore? And, dear Lord, what is this thing?

So after two weeks or more of wondering, I got an appointment to discuss this monster with my doctor. "It doesn't belong there," he says. "I could take it out, but maybe we ought to watch it for a few days, etc..."

So he gives me antibiotics, I wait a week. I go back for the verdict, and he would really like to see it better. So we schedule a CAT scan.

Then I go to the hospital for the CAT scan. I wait in one room, then I get transferred to another room, and then the x-ray machine breaks down. Someone goes for a replacement part for it. You probably know the routine.

And I am not afraid, not one bit! But suddenly, I want to cry. Did you every hear anything so silly? I have no idea why I would want to cry or what about. But I noticed my heart was pounding, my pulse racing and a general heaviness in my chest area. I'm not in pain. I'm not on any kind of medication.

As I sat there and tried to figure out what was going on, I remembered one time a dentist gave me Novocain before extracting a tooth and I felt weepy then!

So I sat there, counting the minutes. I watch as people go by me up and down the halls. I look at the signs, arrows pointing, lines traversing the halls, all going somewhere. On one wall is a nice picture of a cool lake, trees waving in the breeze, blue skies, all a very pleasant scene but it doesn't seem to touch me. I'm in my own little world with all of these questions going through my mind. What am I afraid of?

Then I begin to realize what I'm feeling is a very subtle kind of evil. It has invaded my mind and then goes for my spirit. I WAIT! I PRAY!

I did not communicate with this evil. Neither did I invite him in. I feel like I'm battling something in the upper regions. It is not natural. So as I recognize who and what I'm dealing with, I give him a name and an origin. His name is FEAR. He comes from darkness.

He came uninvited and plans to stay until I am completely in his grip! Well, we can't have that, can we? So I decide to pray...until... "Lord, give me strength. Flood my being with a newfound confidence in your promises to me. You said you'd never leave me nor forsake me. I need you, right now, Lord! Let your peace flood my spirit until I have strength to hold steady until this storm passes."

And you know what? He did!

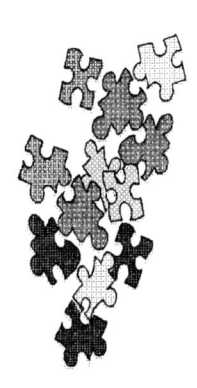

I Feel Special Today

I awakened to what seemed like a very ordinary day. It didn't take long to realize it was far from ordinary! For on this day, August 2, God allowed me (Can you believe this?) to share a little with Him in His creation activities. Please don't panic, I'll explain, hopefully!

We humans, in general, take so many things for granted. Flowers, for instance. I love flowers and always have something blooming in my yard, from the first tiny crocuses that push their winter blankets of snow off their faces, till the snow covers the last of the chrysanthemums in late fall. I often boast about my flowers. I love all flowers. I'm always thanking God for sharing them with me. Counting the flowers, there is much beauty in the world! Plenty for everyone, I'd say.

I was trimming my flower vases this morning, taking out the wilted blossoms and adding new ones, when I was suddenly drawn to the gladiolas. There are so many colors and combinations of color! So I took a second and closer look. I was a little bit surprised at what I saw. It was a little like staring into the face of God.

I don't mean to speak lightly of God, but it did make me think of Him. This flower is so perfect in every way. The deeper I looked into this flower, the more I was aware of the goodness of God. I was mesmerized.

Then my mind was turned to Rwanda in Africa, Bosnia in Europe, I remembered the Cubans taking to the open sea in tubs, fleeing the oppression of their homes, looking for freedom. And there is Somalia and the Kurds to worry about. Khadafi is still in Libia, Houssin in Iraq. There is war and hunger and oppression in the land. There is family violence against women, child abuse against the weak little ones, divorce, abortion and welfare fraud. And God is concerned about all of these things. But tell me, has He ever, just once, forgotten to make the bulbs sprout, the plants to grow and the blossoms to appear in their appointed time? And He does all that just to make me, and others, extremely happy!

Can you imagine living in The Garden of Eden before man fell and the whole order of things was changed, the way God first created it? Imagine the unearthly beauty of it all before Satan got his "I will" attitude and made a big mess of things.

But not to worry! God is still in control! He still sends the rain and the sun. We still enjoy seed time and harvest. And while He is concerned about wars, floods, crime, tornadoes, earthquakes and such, He has never skipped a season of birds singing, flowers blooming and all the beauty He created for our enjoyment.

So while we are all on a journey, let me suggest you slow down and enjoy the beauty all around and realize God is no farther away than your fingertips.

Yes, I am a very lucky person! He shares all of this with me! It must be that He loves me a lot and that MAKES ME SPECIAL!

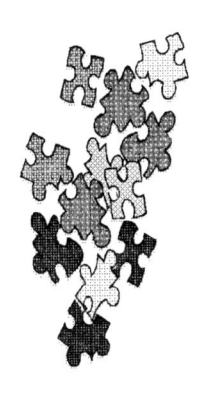

Little Christopher

It's been over two years now, and I still find my eyes wet and my heart aching for you, at times. I'm not sure what brings your face up before me, but often I find it there, a shimmering glow, kind of ethereal, hard to define. But the feelings are very real! We all loved you so very much, Christopher. We expected to enjoy you for years and years, even forever. A lifetime of love was waiting for you. But who can know the future?

Due to a bit of carelessness on the part of one, our whole world has changed. And even now, though we know you are safe at home with our loving Father and you'll never know sorrow or pain, we still feel a terrible loss and loneliness.

In our selfishness we often wish you were here. In our heart of hearts, we know you are safer there. I guess the bottom line is this, even though you weren't allowed to live, nevertheless, you had to die! And I think I shall forever ask, why?

I'm glad I got to hold you, once. It made you feel more a part of me. Great-grandma certainly plans to see you in Heaven, little boy. Until then, please know that we love you!

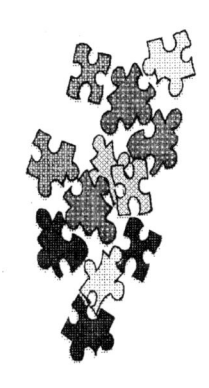

Looking to the Skies, But With Different Eyes

The days are hot in Arkansas in the summer time! Most everyone knows that. So I'm writing a story about such a day, a long time ago.

I awakened this morning, April 2, 1999 with an old 1931 re-run going over and over in my wonderfully sound mind. So after I had watched the news and had my prayer time and this scene was still playing in my head, I figured God wanted me to write it down for some reason or some one. So hang on, here goes.

I remember where we lived every year since 1924, and that's the only way I can remember the times of my life so clearly. On October 17, 1930 my folks had a baby boy. In July 1931 he died. I was nearly ten years old, and I plainly recall my mother crying an awful lot. I had grieved as a child, but had soon gotten on past the worst part of it. We kids found it very depressing to hear her crying and sobbing all the time. Little did I know then, and still don't know, the pain of losing a child. And I'm so glad I don't.

The days were long, we worked hard and after the evening meal was over and the chores all done, we kids played outside till near dark. It was cooler on the

East side of the house. There was no danger to us in those days. Not many kids were stolen, certainly not poor kids.

As I always had trouble with which end should be up and which down, I created my own way to deal with it. I would put my head down and flip my feet up against the side of the house and have my own view of the world around me. It all looked so different from the upside-down position. Now I didn't know what astrology or astronomy meant. I only knew something called to me from the sky.

My mother had some head knowledge about the Bible. She had told us about Abraham, Noah, Jonah, Samson, Jesus, etc. I thought these stories were true but since I couldn't see any trace of them when I stood on my head and searched the sky, I didn't worry about heaven or feel any concern about it. I was just interested in my immediate tomorrow.

We grew up, things changed and one day I realized I was keeping my head up and my feet down and I'm not studying the sky as I once had. But that's okay too. I guess Mama had told me a million times or more, "Keep you dress down. It's not ladylike for a girl to stand on her head all the time." I finally figured it out. Mothers just don't want you to have any fun at all.

Now it's 1943, there's a war going on, I am twenty-two years old and I come face to face with decision time. I heard of Jesus and I believed in Him, but what will I do about it? Well, I didn't waste any time. I accepted Him and a new life started for me. Now I'm seeing through the same eyes I've always had, but I'm seeing through brand new lenses. Everything has changed. All is different. My world has turned upside-down, but this time my head is in the clouds and my feet are still firmly planted on the ground.

As the years continue to pass there are many changes. The world is totally different from the one I grew up in. Human values have changed. And our bodies change also. Our eyesight diminishes somewhat and we grow weak in our bodies. But as my earthly strength begins to fail, my spirit grows stronger. My eyes are set on a higher plane. Now, with my different attitude and purpose, I am losing sight of some earthly things, leaving them behind. And as my spiritual eye becomes clearer and more focused it seems I can almost see my ultimate tomorrow.

And I find my tomorrow is much closer than when I first believed!

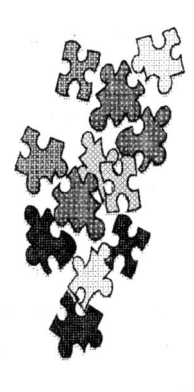

Let It Snow

I'm not sure why I got up this morning thinking about snow. It may have something to do with the fact that my car has not been out of my driveway since Wednesday night, or it might be the weather forecast on TV that says we have over twelve inches of snow on the ground and a possibility of up to six inches more today. Something got my attention and I began to think about snow!

It is so totally beautiful to me. It hides a lot of wintertime ugliness. And it comes in a number of different vehicles. These last three or four days, it has arrived on little furry kitty cat paws. Just as quiet as a mouse.

But sometimes, when there are little sleet-balls mixed in, it hammers on the windows like small firecrackers exploding in the distance. The sound of it puts a chill in your body, even if the house is warm. This snow usually comes in on a brisk wind vehicle.

Then there is the snow that rides in on what is called flurries. It is deposited on my patio and before I've finished admiring it's beauty, another flurry rushes in, grabs it up and takes MY snow over into the neighbor's yard or across the street or who knows where it was taken. Now I'm back to a nearly clean patio. Bummer! But not to worry, the flurries are not finished for today—or this week—or the winter of '96. I've a feeling there will be lots more snow before warm weather arrives.

Sometimes snow comes in like a cheetah at seventy miles an hour. It doesn't look dangerous when viewed from your window, but walk outside and around the corner of your house and it can take you off your feet! Snow is such an innocent-looking thing. You pick up a handful and it so quiet and harmless, so beautiful. It's loads of fun to play in. Most kids love it. (I love to eat it.)

It's here for a purpose, but beware. You must check what vehicle it's arriving on before you plan your activities for the day. Being dressed properly is of great importance if you mean to enjoy this most beautiful time of the year.

God sends it. We need it. So I say, LET IT SNOW!

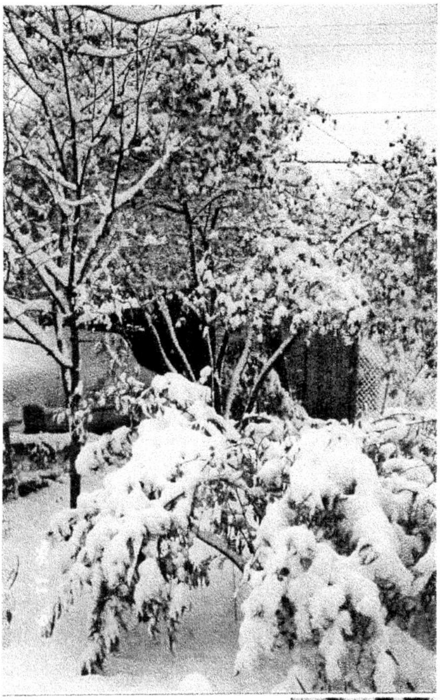

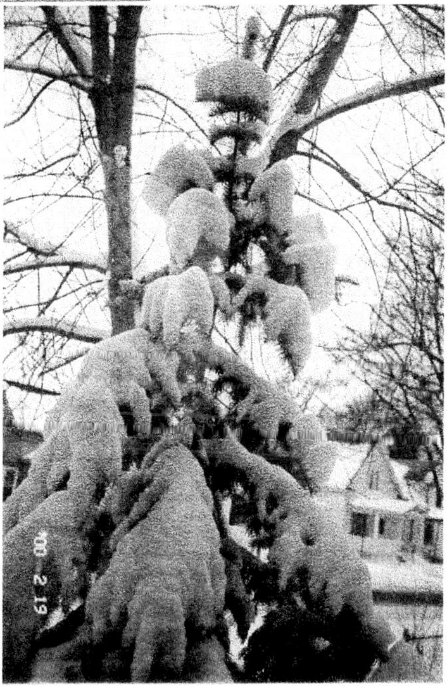

240/MY LIFE IN BITS 'N' PIECES

Snowflakes look like tiny white shields when photographed during a snowstorm!

Memorial Day 1996

As I drove down the streets of my hometown today, I saw and heard bands playing, people marching, crowds milling around, police directing traffic and lots and lots of American flags. As I drove by the cemetery on 16th Street, the brightly colored and freshly planted flowers caught my eye. Very pretty indeed! But the most distinctive colors were the red, white and blue of our nation's flag.

What I'm writing next is not meant for criticism, it's just an observation. One person's perspective. As I was struck by the profusion of color one particular bit of color stood out from all the rest. It was the flags!

Now I know why flags fly at this time of the year, I'm not dumb. I believe this custom began soon after the Civil War. It was called Decoration Day. It was mainly a time of remembering our war dead. And that was good. But how could one forget, is my question? I had a brother who served four years in the South Pacific during World War II. He lived to be a middle-aged man and then died in 1988. And it doesn't take a rose or a marigold or a flag to remind me of him.

I remember a long lifetime of love and sharing and just plain enjoying each other's company. But you know what? This time of year I'm out there making a large pot of flowers to put on his grave, just like everybody else. I sometimes wonder about this custom. We don't do it for the deceased, we do it for ourselves. It makes us feel good! And since the deceased never object, I guess it's all right. But as far as this being a means of remembering my brother, NEVER! There's not a day that passes that I don't think of him. And I treasure my memories.

Written in memory of my brother Billy B. Underwood S 1st Class

Born: August 10, 1924
Died: April 7, 1988

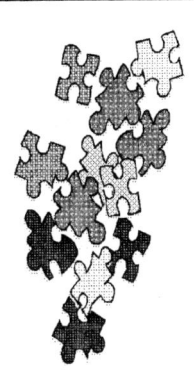

Precious Memories

Once a long time ago, a way out in the country at least ten miles from the nearest town and without any kind of transportation, we spent many evenings at home around our heating stove finding our own entertainment. This was a wintertime scene. The crops are harvested, the groceries are laid up for winter and there's just not much to do. Not even a checker or card game. In some homes where there are several members of the family living together, as was often the case (uncles, cousins, grandparents and the like), you could nearly always get up a checker game, especially among the male population.

But we were different. We lived alone, Father, Mother, two sisters and one brother. We didn't know the game well enough to keep our dad's interest very long. And since my dad had, at one time in the past, had a slight addiction to gambling, no cards were allowed in our house. Besides, who could afford a deck of cards? They probably cost twenty or thirty cents and money was scarce!

This was in the days before electricity in rural areas, 1926 or 1927, and we relied on kerosene lamps after dark. Unlike others who had a lamp in every room, we always seemed to have one lamp. Mama carried it around from room to room when she had to look for something. So for obvious reasons, we tried to always get our chores done, supper over and the dishes done before dark. The outside chores consisted of bringing in enough wood for both stoves, pumping two or three extra pails of water, and feeding all the livestock, which most of the time was a few dozen chickens, a big fattening hog, a cow and a team of work animals, either horses or mules.

Now, with everything done, we were ready to relax for the evening. And there's absolutely nothing to do! No TV, no radio, no Atari games, no books or newspapers. Nothing! But not to worry. My dad had a plan. Now for the memories that are precious.

My father was from a very musical family. His father taught music, and so did my father. It was called, "The First Ten Rudiments of Music," I think. My dad was always singing and whistling. I picked it up very early in life.

So here we sit around in the dark, with only the flickers of light that emanate from the hearth of our heating stove, and Dad says, "Why don't we sing something?" When no one responds he says, "I bet you all know *Amazing Grace*, don't you? Or how about *The Old Rugged Cross*? Or *Shall We Gather At the River*?" So he starts to sing and, one by one, we jump in and sing. And as we go, we get louder. We are in the dark, remember? We don't have to look anyone in the face, so we kind of loose our bashfulness and begin to enjoy ourselves.

Dad knew a zillion songs! Sometimes it woud be *Frankie and Johnny* or *Casey Jones* or *John Henry the Steel Driving Man*. My favorite one was, "In the pines, in the pines, where the sun never shines." It was a good'n!

But there was one problem. My dad could sing high or low or anywhere in between, and I could only sing low, even as a child! I loved singing with him and never tired of it but often I could not reach the high notes, so I'd drop down a bit and keep singing. I'd never heard the word harmonize and this was before he taught me to sing alto, so I feared I was doing something wrong. But it sounded good to me so I kept singing. But I did sing softly. I loved my dad and this was a way to be close to him.

So in the dark in the night we sang. Then as the others grew tired and dropped out, pretty soon I could be heard more clearly. Is it any wonder with three sopranos and one alto? But I didn't try to be heard. I was just doing all I knew how to do and improvising when necessary. But Dad did hear me. He had this ear for music. I remember hearing him say to mom, "Ruth, did you hear that?" And she would say, "Did I hear what?" Then he told her to listen and started another song. After another verse and a chorus he said, "Did you hear it that time?" You'd have to have known my mother to understand her next answer. "How could I hear anything with you and the kids making all that noise?" Can you believe she called our music noise?

Well, Dad eventually figured out that I was the culprit, and he was so glad that one of his offspring seemed to be showing a little talent for something he loved so very much. Thus began my education in doe, re, mi. We had shaped notes in our songbooks back in those days.

This gave me a closeness with Dad the others did not have, for they did not enjoy singing as I did. I treasured this bond and was even known to boast about it on occasions, if you get my drift!

As I grew older we sang at school functions, Tri-county Conventions, churches or anyplace we were asked to sing. Many times, as I grew up, my dad would call me and say, "Hey, Jimmy, I've got these new stamps-Baxter Songbooks. You want to try a few new songs?" Don't ask me why I was called "Jimmy," for I never knew. It was just one of those things. Anyway, I never questioned when Dad called. I ran and we sang. It may have been the extra attention that I needed, and I loved it. This memory is precious!

And I think of a scripture to go with everything. 1 Kings 19:11 & 12 says God was not in the thunder and lightening or any of the other catastrophes, but was in the still, small voice.

And in my case, it was the voice I tried to keep still and small that finally got attention. Isn't that odd?

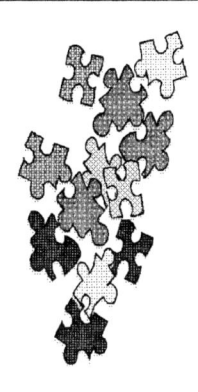

Keeper of the Flame

Our pastor is so cool! Recently he talked about a bulldog anointing. I thought it was real funny but, at the same time, very serious business. Which brings me to the story I'm about to write.

First, let me explain what is meant by "bulldog anointing," if I can. I think it means an anointing that changes you, will not quit, one you can't get away from, one that compels you to act. In short, you can run but you can't hide. A feeling of do or die, sort of. Do you think I'm being too melodramatic? Seriously, I get thoughts running through my head at times that take on that bulldog quality.

As I sat in church Sunday, enjoying the sermon immensely, a thought came into my mind—four words to be exact, and they wouldn't let go. It had absolutely nothing to do with the sermon. "Keeper of the flame" is what I heard. I sat in amazement, wondering what it meant. And since it continued to bounce around in my head, I decided to scribble it down in my book, so I wouldn't forget it. Not that I would EVER forget anything!

So here it is Monday morning and it's still on my mind, so I sit down to try to make sense of it.

My very first thought had to do with the eternal flame at President John Kennedy's grave in Arlington Cemetery, Washington D.C. But why would I be reminded of this flame? Seeing it is taken care of by someone who has been paid in advance, probably. The Kennedy's can afford something like this.

But I'm pretty certain God is not interrupting my concentration on the sermon to focus my mind on the flame that burns on the Kennedy grave. Why would He? No, there's more to this than that! So I begin to try to figure out what is being said to me.

As a "poet" I often think in poetic terms. Such as: The flame of life grows dim in the ill and aging person. On the other hand, we see the young person trying to do everything, go everywhere, try every new trick, and we say, "They are burning the candle (flame) at both ends." And there's the Christian parents whose children are growing up too swiftly, they see their kids getting too close to the questionable things and they intensify their commitment and prayer life for the safety of their children. Later in life these same children will say it was the steadfast, Christian flame like a beacon, like a magnet that kept drawing them back to safety.

Now that I have established the real or mythical flame as an absolute in our lives, the question is, "Who keeps it alive?" Is it God's job to see that the flame is fed and kept burning? Can we just relax and assume that God will do everything for us? Or, is it our responsibility to keep going back to the well, time and time again, for a refill? Aren't we warned to have extra oil for our lamps just in case the wait is longer than expected?

It seems to me we are given a small flame of God's light when we receive Jesus as our Lord and, as we grow and stay very near to Him, our flame grows. And as we share our light with others, it never diminishes, it only grows brighter.

So I guess we are basically the keeper of our own flame. But not to forget the help of the Lord, our supply!

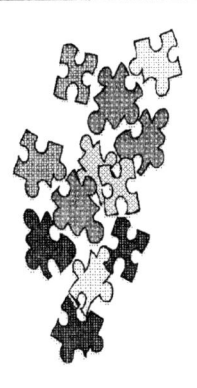

The Watchman

The eagle sits high upon a limb of a tree overseeing the forest around him. His eyes, his vision is far reaching. Nothing moves that he does not see it. He sits so still that, at a glance, you might wonder why does he sit thus? Nothing moves. He looks like a statue in stone. Not even the eyes move (we think). But wait. How could he see the tiny movement in the grass many hundreds of feet below, where the hare and rodent usually go? They too, must be about their business of looking for food. They are part of the chain!

And in spite of all appearances, the watchman's eyes see all. He plummets to the earth in a flash and never misses a target! Then, back to the nest he goes, taking his lunch with him. This is called "mission accomplished." It's like stopping at Burger King or Mickey Dee's for me!

Now, I've always been an admirer of Edgar Allen Poe. He speaks of a stately bird of Yore, perched upon the bust of Pallas, high above his chamber door. But this was not an eagle! Oh, no! Dire as it's message was and stately as it sat, it was no eagle. Why do you suppose the eagle was chosen for a symbol for the United States of America?

The eagle does not become a pet. He does not sit upon a gloved hand and go fetch! He is ruler of all he oversees. He bows to none. He is fierce in all and someone to be reckoned with, if you are a hare, rodent, fox or some other animal in the forest. He represents strength, ability and staying power! His head is white, his eyes are red with his own particular kind of lust. And with the blue sky high about him, he makes a good representative for the United States of America. I couldn't have made a better choice.

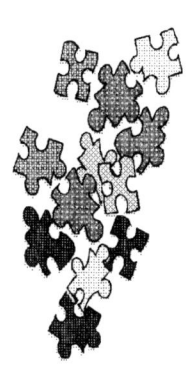

A Song of Thankfulness

Our country celebrates Thanksgiving on November 26 this year, and I think that is great! In the fall I start looking forward to this very happy holiday. Nearly all of my family comes home for this occasion. They all bring their families and food, and together we have a great day. I've lived here nearly thirty years, so I've made lots of friends. Usually several come that are not relatives. And it would not be complete without them. But in the midst of all the celebration with families, friends and food I'm reminded of other reasons to be thankful.

I remember a night in 1943 when I walked (scared to death) down an aisle to an altar and gave my heart to the Lord.

I remember the many pitfalls He helped me through when, by myself, I would have failed.

I remember the good health He has given me and I've enjoyed for seventy-seven years.

I'm aware of all the good people He's situated in my path, in certain places, when He knew I would be needing aid and comfort.

And I've always been blessed with a good attitude. I can always see the hand of God in every situation. I have no use for negativity! The day may be dark and cloudy, but I know the sun is just as bright as usual. I just can't see it. All is still well with my soul. I will not fear! I'm not alone! God's still on His Throne.

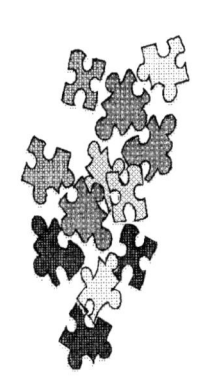

I Love Things That Are Green

Oh, how "ruled by habit" we become as we age! I started this day as I do every day, but somehow today seemed a little different.

Now everybody knows that elderly people do not care for change. Take me, for instance. I've often said, "I don't want any surprises." Not that I'd be considered elderly by any stretch of the imagination!

So this morning I rise at my usual time, make my coffee, take care of my cat named Dawg, brush my teeth, get my cup of coffee and sit down to see what's on the news. Now, I don't watch just any news. It is NBC News. And why, you may ask, does it have to be NBC News? Well, I know these people. I know their spouses, their children, where they live and where they came from. I've amassed a lot of info about these people. I know them!

So I sit on my couch, in my certain and very comfortable spot, and now I'm ready for the day. So now, my favorite news team begins to tell me what is happening in our world, both the good and the bad things.

So now, I try to explain the "green" in my title. I wish I could write this in such a way that you could feel what I'm feeling. I look to my left and see many colors of green. Did you know that there are literally hundreds of different shades of green? I'm looking at a large, spiny cactus plant that is a great mixture of shades of green. Darker body, lighter spines and still lighter leaves. This plant is at least three feet tall and so intricately put together. Only God could make a cactus! I call this guy Geronimo. I think its real name is Totem Pole Cactus. And just beyond this guy is a monkey tail cactus, hanging in the window. All green! It has a million little prickers on it and long ragged spires hanging or growing in every direction.

On the table stands a white orchid. The body is green. This will be a challenge as I have never had an orchid before. And there's another plant in that same window. I don't know the name of it, but it's a beauty. It's green (of course) but with shades of purple on the backs of the leaves. It has hints of purple on the top side also. Real neat!

Then my eye travels, from left to right, and I see a cascading waterfall of philodendron, from ceiling to floor. All shades of green. One plant even has marbling of light green, nearly silver, throughout it. Great!

Then, as my eyes travel along, I reach the window in the south side of the house. And, guess what? There's more green to be seen. Inside the window there's a Norfork Pine. Or is it, Norfolk pine? Now we take a turn, outside the house, and I never leave my couch.

Just outside this window is a blue spruce tree, but it's green. This is my pride and joy. A stately tree, it was a gift from a friend who checked out of this life a few years ago, and a lot too soon. And mixed with this spruce is a Mimosa Tree, sharing the same space. Now, the Mimosa is a tree from the deep South and is therefore late in getting green. But it will be green.

From there I look further to the right, and I'm now looking on my glassed-in front porch. And here my eyes are literally assailed by every shade of green, because my porch houses nearly one hundred houseplants. From where I sit I can see a Palm tree, an Angel Wing Begonia, Asparagus Fern, Spider plant, English Ivy, Mother-In-Laws Tongue, Air Root plant, just to mention a few.

Beyond this window I see big trees—Oak, Elm and Maple and a Yew! And the wind is playing tag with the branches. As the limbs, leaves and branches move in rhythm with the wind, I catch a glimpse of light that must be the white house across the street from me. Sometimes there is a blur I see through the dancing of the tree limbs, and it's a car going by on 17th Street. And you know what...? The overall color is green!

Now I pass across the scene, on to my right, and there's another south window. And here I see, at a quick glance, a Lady Fern, Christmas Cactus, Joseph's Coat, a Jade plant, a potted Begonia, two African Violets, one pink and one purple, but the plants are green. Imagine that!

Now we are by the west window and it's covered by three large plants—A variegated Air Root plant, an Umbrella plant and a funny looking one that I don't have a name for. And just outside this window is a purple leaf Plum tree and another Maple. And would you believe they are all green!

Earlier this morning there was a light rain or mist coming down to add to the beauty of the scene. Can you imagine, for a moment a mischievous God, romping in and among His creation, just enjoying the beauty of it? And I sometimes imagine He did it all just for my enjoyment!

So as I watch this little performance going on outside my windows, my heart swells up with love for Him and my eyes brim over with the emotions I'm feeling. The nearness of God! His love for me! And vice-versa. I just love being able to praise Him for all He does for us, and for all the lovely shades of green. I'm reminded of "Gorillas in the Mist," and it's all here, before my eyes...except the gorillas. And I can live without the gorillas, I believe.

What Brought This On?

Where do all the old folk go,
When there is no where to go?
They just sit and reminisce
About things of long ago.

Like I'm doing now. Recently, while some of my daughters were doing some interior work in one of my bedrooms upstairs, one of them reminded me of some things that happened long ago. And I couldn't get it out of my mind, so I'll write it down. Call it part of my memories.

My husband never went to church with me. And, having had seven children, my hands were full.

I did not send or take my children to the nursery. I kept them in church with me. Oh, I'd go change a diaper or feed a baby or, once in a while, I'd take one of the older ones to the nursery to scold them or downright threaten them if they were being bad. But otherwise they sat like blackbirds on a telephone wire near me!

And like all mothers, I knew which ones could not be trusted to not touch one another. So I had a system for seating. I held Quaita on my lap, she was the least. Then I sat Melodi on my left side, away from any conflict that might break out. She was next in age to the baby. Now, I've got three more that have to be strategically placed for various reasons. In this three, there are two who need a lot of oversight, if you know what I mean! So through trial and error I finally worked out a system that I thought was working very well.

Holly, being the next youngest and also being one of the two afore mentioned who needed a lot oversight, I put her on my right side next to me. Then comes Star, next in age and one who gave me little trouble (out in public), so I sat her to the right of Holly. Now it seems that things are falling in place. That only leaves Billy, who is the oldest of these five, so he is placed on Star's right. The oldest two have already quit going to church. And I think I have a system that works.

Can't you just imagine the sight? Every Sunday, in I come, herding my brood to the pew, getting everybody in his or her place. Then I settle back to hear what God has for me through the minister's mouth. And I need the word of God so badly, for these are very difficult years. I have no help it seems. Not financially, not physically and most certainly not spiritually. No help! So I dearly need all the church I can get.

So while I'm trying to follow the pastor's words, I'm also trying to keep my eyes on the kids as best as I can. I'm sort of in the midst of the twain! Often as we left church my pastor would say, "Sister Key, you have the best-behaved children in the house." Now I am so proud. So I pat myself on the back and go home happy.

And now, thirty-five years later, I get the complete story. Star, who is the good kid that I put between the two bad kids, tells me, "Mom, those two kids nearly beat me to death on a regular basis." And it was always behind my back, so I couldn't see what was going on. Star really jerked the rug out from under me. So there goes my assurance that I was doing a good job! And now I'm back to 1964, struggling with a bunch of normal kids, thinking I'm doing a decent job of bringing them up right.

And now to find out later, I was being duped by the most angelic faces you'd ever want to see.

And I thought I was smart!

Myself with six of the seven
Left to right: Billy, Gina, Roy Jr., Me holding Melodi, Star and Holly

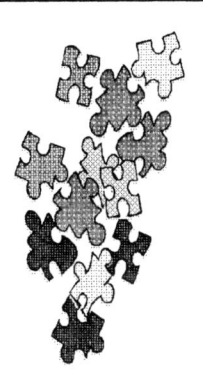

I Have a Confession

Not that you'll believe I have a fault or shortcoming, but I'll tell you anyway! Most of you, at least some of you, know that I have a large family. And you may know that I've never, ever lived alone until Thanksgiving week, 1998. Living alone is NOT a good thing! I know it comes to that as people grow older and their children grow up, marry and leave home. But, in my opinion, there ought to be a law against it!

Several years ago, 1976 to be exact, I returned to school and learned a lot of stuff. I learned how to do algebra, had my mind re-activated as to world events in general. Sociology and health became a new challenge to me. I took every class I could find time for, but there was no class or training on what's referred to as "empty nest syndrome." There are no shots to prevent this disease. It can get anyone, I suspect, and it is more widespread than most people think or know. So what's a body to do?

My house only has three bedrooms, so I can't move seven families back in with me. There are now thirteen grandchildren and two great-grandchildren, which poses a problem, as I don't have enough room for them to play in my tiny yard. Besides, I'd beat them if they stepped on my flowers and stuff. And I do have lots of stuff in my yard! Actually I have fourteen trees that are large enough to make a shade and there are thirty Mimosa trees, all the way from one inch high to some that will blossom this year. But that's another story in itself. The Mimosa Garden! Another time!

Back to the empty nest story. You couldn't hire my kids to move back, even if there was room for them, because I am the boss here and they all want to be the boss, too. Where did they get that attitude?

So I'm back to, lots of room or wide-open spaces or whatever you call it. I just know one thing—I don't like it! Believe me, I do try not to lean on my kids or cling to them, too much. I try very hard not to need them, but I do.

So I sit her alone, and remember the days when everybody needed me and there wasn't enough of me to go around comfortably. And then my greatest enemy begins to take advantage of my wandering mind and I find myself thinking, "If I had anything they needed they'd be here." Self-pity is an ugly thing!

These last eight or ten days have been worse than usual, as I hurt my back and I've been hampered in my everyday activities. Like working in the yard, which is how I hurt my back in the first place! Understand, I'm not down, just slowed down.

So this so-called pal of mine visits me a lot. I call him, Pity. He's here in the morning and also here at night when I go to bed. He's beginning to bother me. I know I can't give in, so I begin to pray. Now, isn't it funny how when one prays, things happen? I'm often surprised myself, how long it takes for me to remember this. Not that I don't pray (a lot) about a lot of other things and other needs.

But this brings me to Tuesday, June 15, 1999. My son-in-law called mid-morning or so and asked if he could come by, bring lunch and eat with me. Well, that sure gave my spirit a boost. Then he came back, at dinnertime and brought my evening meal. He didn't eat with me this time, because it was too early for him because of his work. Didn't keep me from eating though. So Melodi came by for a short visit that same day. Mid afternoon my oldest daughter-in-law, Kathy, came by for an hour or so, and we had a great time catching up on what's happening with them. Then on top of all that, my daughter, Quaita, and her daughter, Ashley, came over and brought me a new bedspread and visited until 8:30 p.m. Wow, what a day!

Needless to say, I went to bed a very happy person. And I didn't forget to thank God for my joyful day. You know, He always provides for my every wish and need If I Let Him!

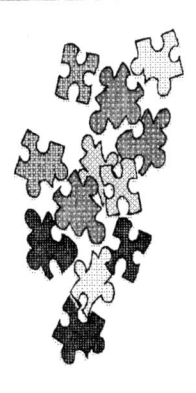

Mostly Fiction

'Tis the night before surgery and I'm not afraid, even though I know this nice young doctor is going to slice off my shoulder, fix whatever is wrong on the inside of it, sew it back onto my body and hope in a few months it will work again.

"There is nothing to be afraid of," they say. "It's not life-threatening," others say. This huge gash the doctor will cut across my lovely body will only be about a foot long and there will be only about 3,942 and ½ stitches in it. And it will be at least four inches from my heart, so not to worry. I tell myself I'm going to be okay in a few months! As good as new, I'll bet, probably better.

So, it if is all so simple, why am I counting the hours? You see, I've already had my last meal before, you know...! Now I'm wondering if I shouldn't have had a nicer meal. After all, a condemned man in prison gets a real good meal before he dies, and I'm wondering if I'll regret not having had the very best when I wake up, IF I wake up!

So now they give me something to relax me and make me sleepy. Why is it that doctors and nurses make sure you are sound asleep before they come at you with evil intent? You can't even fight back! And this doesn't seem exactly fair, does it?

And so, I begin to drift off on a big cloud. But before I go, I start wondering...Did I have someone's name on my will and on my checking account? And...Did I pay my house and car insurance? And...then...

I w o n d e r.........H
                      O
                   W L
                      O
                      N
                      G T
                 W   H
                  I   O
                   L   S
                    L L   E G
                     A   R
                     S   O
                      T #   C
                         !   E
                        ??   R
                         *   I
                        @   E
                         $ S

                          !

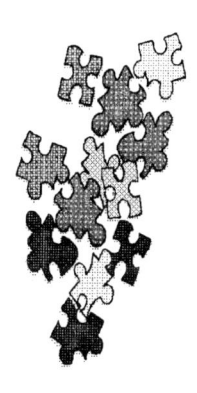

Am I Allowed One Big Mistake?

I think it speaks volumes for a person to give such a little thought to a matter of such importance. I'm not sure today, forty-seven years after the fact, why I married my husband. I had not been saved very long. I didn't know God had stated plainly we are not to be unequally yoked together with unbelievers. But not knowing does not change the word of God. So payday came early and remained for a very long time.

I didn't know, for forty years, how to forgive myself. I know God had forgiven me, but it was much harder forgiving myself. It was a wonderful day in my life when Romans 8:1 (There is therefore now no condemnation to them which are in Christ Jesus, who walk not after the flesh, but after the Spirit.) became a reality to me. And even after we are forgiven for our sins, mistakes or our past, we often find we must live with the results of our poor decisions. And this is right and just, for God is a just God! People should be very careful about their plans to marry. I wish they would ask me first!

And after having said all that I'll attempt to write about my life with my husband. I got married on August 12, 1946 in Manila Arkansas. We were out riding around for no particular reason, just cruising, when we passed a Baptist church and parsonage. Since we had the marriage license with us, we just stopped, went in and asked the minister to marry us and he did. Wasn't that romantic? We started married life in the home of his relatives!

Did we have a honeymoon? Not hardly! Did we have good weather? Sure, it was cotton-picking weather. It was about 95° to 100° at noontime in August, in Arkansas. Did we take pictures? No. Did we spend a lot of money? What is money? Were my spouse and I a lot alike? Are you kidding? Did I find marriage difficult? Very! This could go on forever.

Within the first year my first son was born. Roy Francis Key, Jr. arrived on May 16, 1947, and then my life became much better. I had someone who loved me unconditionally. He became my entire life. My world revolved around this little guy. I don't recall much about the husband after the boys' arrival, and I probably wasn't a very good wife. But of course, I didn't have a very good husband either. He started drinking and staying away from home on a regular basis. He spent every dime we made in the cotton fields on women and drinks. Great marriage, wouldn't you say?

This continued for seventeen years and six more children. When the seventh child was six months old, he finally left us, went back to Arkansas. People asked me why I stayed with him or why I didn't divorce him. I didn't have to search for my answer. I always thought, "until death do us part" meant just that. I never accepted divorce as a viable alternative. I couldn't see how God could get any glory from me running out of a situation He had nothing to do with getting me into. And since two mistakes do not erase the one, I stayed! I had made a commitment and I would honor it if it killed me. And it nearly did, at times.

He was not a physical wife beater! But he nearly killed us with his neglect. We looked like gypsies. We ate very poorly. My pride, which I had in abundance, suffered tremendously! The church we attended fed us part of the time. We wore their hand-me-down clothes. Humiliation was my steady diet. Even when I was thankful for their help, it was not their problem. It was mine, or should have been.

And after Roy Sr. left us in 1964, God literally fed us day by day, for a period of time that I had to wait before I could draw A.D.C. from the state! That also was a bitter pill for me to swallow, but I had to have it for the children's sake. When God sent us food, I was torn between rejoicing and humiliation. To sum it all up I'd say, "my pride took a licking, but kept on ticking." I have to be very careful about pride. It can be an ally or an enemy. My father always told us not to accept anything we couldn't pay for, so I was in a bad spot. He was a very proud man, and he passed it down to me!

I think I was a rather strict parent. I knew how I wanted my children to act, and I insisted on obedience. I kept my children in church. I disciplined with love, I think. My pastor called me, "old Faithful."

Sometimes you hear people say, "If I could go back and do it over"—how they would change. I doubt that I'd change any of the things I did! I still believe "if you bring them up in the way you'd have them go, when they are old they will not depart from it." I insisted on honesty and truthfulness, people helping people, sharing the burden. It works for me!

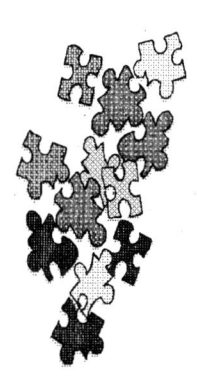

Same Song—Second Verse

Because of this attempt to write the story of my life, I have been thinking a lot on the past. It often runs through my mind like an old movie rerun. I am relaxed and it just flows by, real peaceful like, most of the time. But on occasion I get stuck with a thought that struggles to come forth, something forgotten for a while and I have to really "dig" for it. And there's no one left in my family that I can go to for help in remembering things.

Even though my mother's education was limited, she was a very smart person. I've said, so many times in my life, "Mom, do you remember...?" And she always came up with the information I needed. But she has been gone since July of '73, so my ready source of information is gone. "Thanks, Mom, for all the answers to all the questions."

Now, my older sister, who ought to be able to help me with a few of my questions, is in the mid-stages of Alzheimer's disease, So she's no help at all. I guess I'm on my own!

Oh well, if I could remember every day and every incident of my life, there would not be enough paper and pens, not to mention time, left to write it all down anyway!

So, while doing this serious reminiscing, I've become aware of the fact that I've lived during some very important events in the history of the world. I've decided to rewrite some of my remembrances and add a few things.

I'm afraid I made my life very dull and depressing, but it wasn't all bad. I probably didn't show the whole picture. But since I'm not a professional writer, please forgive my oversight and repeating passages. Maybe I'm allowed two mistakes?

Actually, my life was not all work and drudgery. We didn't have a lot of worldly goods, but we did have two parents who were home every night to take care of whatever needed taking care of. We kids were not aware that we were poor. We were a well-adjusted bunch of kids.

The Great Depression didn't happen overnight. Black Friday that came on October 29, 1929 did not effect us. We had no money in the bank or anywhere else! We had nothing to lose or give up. So we just went from nothing to a little more of the same. No big thing to us. We lived through it, and here I am to prove it and I'm still doing fine. No lingering effects at all.

Now I continue to record some memorable things that happened in my lifetime. I guess I missed World War I by a few years, but I've heard a lot about the times from my folks. My father was the right age to go, but he was married. But they waited for his call anyway, and as they waited he kept working at his job at the local stave mill.

Anyone know what you do at a stave mill? Well, I'll tell you! They make staves! Staves are the individual parts that when connected together become a wooden barrel. And wooden barrels were made to store stuff in. Every home had at least one barrel in it, for they kept their flour in it. And the lid on top of the barrel was called a dough board. It was for rolling your biscuit dough on and for cutting out the biscuits. The dry flour was bought at the grocery store in cotton sacks and it was emptied into the barrel. And every morning and noon, someone made biscuits and cooked them in a large, wood-burning stove.

But back to WW I. My father got a finger cut off at his job just shortly before he was called to be examined for the draft. Understand, many men lost fingers to the sharp saws of the stave mills. It was not uncommon. But a few people questioned the timing of this accident. One man dared to ask my dad about it and got knocked down for his inquisitiveness. Dad hit him with his bandaged hand and had to go back to the doctor and have it sewed up again. He did not like his courage questioned. So the United States had to win that war without the help of my Dad. And they did win it.

As I have already mentioned the Great Depression, I'll go on to the crash and burning of the airship Hindenburg. This happened in 1937, killing 36 people, and putting an end to passenger service for the huge aircraft. This one was 812 feet long and 135 feet in diameter. It flew regular trips to Europe and South America, crossing the Atlantic Ocean 36 times. It crashed and burned on May 6, 1937 as it approached the landing field in New Jersey, coming home from Germany.

We only had a once a week newspaper to keep up with the world events, but my mother managed to keep up with the news. She had a great curiosity about what was happening in other parts of the world. I wonder it that's where I got my great desire to know everything. I want to know everything—then and now!

My youngest sister was born in 1937 also. But the world didn't hear about that. The world didn't hear about my birth either. In fact, not many people know anything about the man who was president of the United States when I was born. Warren G. Harding. Anyone remember him? Now I don't feel too bad about not being known.

Another memorable thing that happened in my lifetime, and I only remember it vaguely, was Charles A. Lindburgh's solo flight from New York City to an airfield near Paris, France. This was on May 20, 1927. It took thirty-three and a half hours. It was on every tongue. It was unheard of. But Lindy did it! I was less than six years old, but I remember!

But what I recall much better was the kidnapping of his little boy in 1932. The little boy was killed, someway, and a new law was passed by congress, making kidnapping a federal crime. It was very traumatic! I remember my mother crying a lot about, "that poor little baby," and his, "poor mother." I don't remember father's being too important to my mother. Not even my Father! I never understood that. Dad was everything to me.

Time continued with a baby brother being born to our family on October 12, 1933. Nothing out of the ordinary going on at this time. We were living much better at this time, financially.

Then we started hearing rumblings of a war in Europe. Most especially, Germany. The name of Hitler kept coming up a lot. And as some of us remember, and the rest of you know from history, World War II began! The consensus of the people was, they can't do that! How can one man influence so many people and wreak such havoc? We couldn't believe our ears. But it did happen, and it was the most horrible time. And the sin against the Jews of Europe was atrocious. It went from bad to absolutely unthinkable! So we consoled ourselves with the fact that it was a long way from Western Europe to the U.S.A. It was their mess, let them deal with it! But that don't fly.

One day, December 7, 1941, we found the war had reached out and dragged us right into the middle of it. No longer could we be complacent about "their" war. It was now, ours, too. In fact, it became my war. My brother, who was nearing seventeen years of age, grew up mighty fast. When he turned eighteen he went into the Navy. He went to San Diego for boot camp, and we didn't see him again for over four years. He didn't get the usual thirty days at home after boot camp, but went straight to the Pacific Theatre of war.

I still have his good conduct ribbons and his battle stars on special ribbons showing what area of the world he served in, especially in relation to the major battles he was involved in. I also have all of the letters he wrote me from the Pacific Islands. They come from the Marianna Groupe, the Carolina Isles, Guam, Pelalu and Islands whose names I've forgotten. These things are sixty years old, but I count them as some of my special treasures.

My brother did come home after the war in pretty good physical shape, after four years in hell that only another service man could understand. He married and fathered five children. He spent the rest of his life driving a long haul truck to support his family quite well.

Then in April of 1988, he died of cancer and that was the greatest loss I've ever suffered and the hurtingest thing I've ever endured. But his death served a double purpose in my life. It brought me back to the Lord from a backslidden state I had existed in for fifteen years. I came back to the Lord for forgiveness and got it. Upon being asked by close friends, when I was coming back to the Lord, I'd say it will probably take something drastic (for Satan holds fast, those that he gets his hands on). He really had a grip on me, but since my brother's death was the ultimate in drastic, it got the job done and I'm so glad. God still works in mysterious ways to get His will done. And I'm grateful!

And I did have a cousin who lost his life on the Battleship Arizona when Pearl Harbor was bombed. "Back to the war again." In later years, in 1968, I believe, his mother got a chance to go visit the monument that was erected atop the superstructure of the Arizona, right where it sank in Pearl Harbor. Did you know there were eighteen ships sunk or severely damaged, about 170 planes and 3,700 men lost in the initial attack on our Navy in that one day? Almost all of the Navy was concentrated in that one area. Our enemies knew it too. Talk about a Black Day in history!

279/MY LIFE IN BITS 'N' PIECES

I suppose there are advantages to having lived over seventy years. There are so many memories. I do remember V.E. Day and V.J. Day and D-Day. I also remember exactly where I was when J. F. Kennedy was shot. That was November 22, 1963. And I was very pregnant with my last child.

I had taken my mother to shop for groceries at Taft's Supermart in South Haven. I stayed in the car for obvious reasons, but I had the radio on. When I heard the announcement about the President's assassination in Dallas, Texas, I ran in the store to tell my mom. I was crying aloud and many others were crying too. They had already heard it. This was hard to deal with since it was repeated over and over. There was all the TV coverage, the reruns, the reenactment and such. The pictures of the President falling over into his wife's lap. Jackie trying to cover his body with her own. Then there was the riderless horse at the funeral and, above all, little Jon Jon's farewell salute to his father. That I'll never forget. It was all so emotion-filled and I was pregnant, so I'm sure that made it worse for me. It really hurt me!

And then I remember Neil Armstrong's walk on the moon! I never thought it was possible but I saw it. What can I say? It was marvelous! But this did not touch me in the way other news had. And too, I didn't sit in front of the TV much, as my husband had left us and I was very busy trying to feed and clothe my kids.

Then in January, 1986 another life-shaking event happened. I'll never forget the explosion of the space shuttle. The twin smoke plumes erupting out of the fireball that had been the Challenger. I can close my eyes and still see it many years later. Etched in my memory for all eternity! All this happened only 75 seconds after launch.

And since then not much has happened. Street gangs killing each other. A host of stolen guns. Tons of illegal drugs. Children being sexually assaulted and killed. Old people killed in their homes. Increased car, plane and train wrecks, and it all seems dull in comparison. It's no wonder preachers are talking of the End time and Last days.

About time, wouldn't you say?

My Views on Retirement

I had a lot of confusing thoughts about retirement. I was afraid about finances. I had married when I was twenty-five years old and spent the next several years having my seven children. I was married in August of 1946 and had my last child in January of 1964. My husband was Roy F. Key, Sr., who was born on November 6, 1917 in Philcampbell, Alabama. We were married in Manila, Arkansas, on August 12, 1946 by a Baptist minister in the church parsonage.

My husband left us in July of 1964 and in 1967 I went to work to support my family. I first worked for Chase Manufacturing Company in Douglas, Michigan and then I got a job at General Electric Company in Holland Michigan. Both were good jobs and that is probably why I was afraid to retire. But when I was sixty-three I retired. It wasn't easy, but I made it work. I live on a lot less but I get by. I pay all my bills on time every time and I haven't lost any weight, so I guess I'm doing okay. Now I have a motto: No job, no man, no problems!

I don't have a lot of leisure time, but when I can I love to read. I have always loved to read. I love all kinds of books and many authors. Plus I read the Bible through every year. I also love poetry.

I love sports too, especially baseball. And I like basketball, too. I try to get over to Detroit two or three times in a season. My sons-in-law would take me anytime I wanted to go. I've got some great in-laws. I watch a lot of Tiger games on TV too. I've got tons of score books with every hit, every run, every error and who hit what into which field. You might say, I became a fanatic. I've been retired over sixteen years now, and I've gone through some changes. Now I write for fun—short stories and poetry.

I would love to travel, but that's not in my budget. Besides, I don't sleep well in some other bed besides mine. I love my waterbed, and I don't find many of those away from home.

I have traveled to New York quite a few times. My daughter, Star, lived in Albany, New York for several years and she paid for my trips out there. While in Albany we would go down to the Big Apple and see a ballgame in Yankee Stadium. New York is a beautiful place to visit but it ought to be against the law for anyone to have to live there. They now live here in Holland, so I have no excuse to go to New York.

I make a trip to Memphis, Tennessee and Trumann, Arkansas about once a year to visit a brother and sister and that's about the extent of my traveling. All of my seven children live within forty miles of me, so I don't need to travel much.

I still keep busy and I don't have time to be lonely. In fact, I don't believe I ever spent one night alone until these last two years. Someone has always lived with me. My one daughter has lived in the house with me all of her life, except for a very little. I also had a son with his girl and boy here for several years, so I didn't get lonely. They have all been gone now for two years, and I do miss them. I still see all of them a lot.

Plus I go to church four or more times a week, regularly, and more if there are special services. For two years I worked one day a week as a caregiver for an elderly lady, but I got tired of that. I found it to be a lot of time and very little pay, so I quit. I'd rather be at home. She was ninety-seven years old and blind. I worked a twenty-four hour shift.

My health is great, for which I am thankful. Naturally there are some activities I've had to stop. I can't climb a tree anymore. I don't jump rope or play hopscotch, either. But I do anything I want or need to do!

Would you believe I can remember living in twenty-six different houses? And I know there were three or four I can't remember. But the best one is where I live now. It's mine! I worked and earned it by the sweat of my brow and with the help of the Lord. It doesn't look so special, but it's special to me. It has everything I need and it accommodates extra people too, so what more could I need?

Now for becoming a grandparent! I was not excited about that. In fact, I wouldn't allow my step-grandchildren to call me gramma. I guess it's more fun now than it used to be. I have thirteen grandchildren and three great-grands. My oldest granddaughter (twenty-three years old now) was a track and field star in school. She was also into gymnastics, running, jumping all the like, and I went to see her perform as often as I could. I go to my other grandchildren's ball games. I have one grandson in football and a few of them are in baseball. I go to all the games I can. My days, weeks and months as a retiree are full and happy times. I love living life!

Sometimes I run into some of my former co-workers from General Electric, and it's like another family. It's always so good to see them. We stop and catch up on things.

And now some advice I would give my children about life. Always do your best. Give your best. Be your best and enjoy your life to the fullest extent! And don't forget to invite God to be a part of it. Take your directions from Him and having done that, there will be no need for saying, "Oh, if only I could go back and do my life over." And having made my share of mistakes, I know of a few I'd like to change, but since I can't, I don't beat myself up about them.

The Bible says in Romans 8:1, There is therefore now no condemnation to them which are in Christ Jesus, who walk not after their flesh, but after the Spirit. I cannot change the past, so I live for today. I'm making the best of it!

I trust God with Death and the Hereafter. Life is good. It's very good!

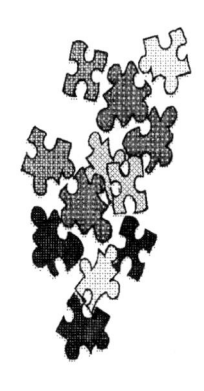

A Great Controversy

I am thinking of middle age when I, by reasons beyond my control, was still young. Would you believe I had three children after the so-called middle-age began? At thirty-five, thirty-nine, and forty-two years of age I had new babies. So how was I to find time to become old or even middle-aged? I figured on getting back to the middle-aged years some time later, if I found time!

As for liking one time in my life better than another, herein lies another controversy. I believe every day is a gift from God, and how can I say I liked one better than another? No gift from God is a bad gift! The difference may well be in how I use the days I've been given. Right now I am able to group some of my days and years together and say, "These were used better, so I enjoyed them more."

After my husband left, when my seventh child was six months old, there was no time for relaxing and enjoying middle age. Two years later I got a job, I lost twenty pounds and looked better than I had looked in twenty years. Nearly! If this all seems hard to believe, refer back the title of this chapter. I did not have time to get wrinkles or gray hair. I was busy feeding a big family and raising them without any help from a father or anyone else. It was not an easy task.

Both of my boys (at different times) got a broken arm as they grew up. One of the girls did too! My oldest son had diphtheria. They all had chickenpox, whooping cough, measles, ear infections, poison ivy, everyday colds, influenza and even head lice. One girl had pneumonia three times in her first year. That's scary! My second son broke his hand, later in life, but he was still at home. This happened in a street fight the night he turned eighteen and could legally drink. And he did! He thought he was grown, I guess. Had a cast on his hand to prove it! This same son broke his foot, sliding into third base, playing softball one summer. While the opposing team kept fumbling the ball in the outfield, he kept running till he neared third base. And here he slid in, and that's where his foot was broken. Then to make the play more dramatic, he got up and hopped home. Was this good offense or bad defense? You make the call!

I always loved sports, so I was at a game nearly every night for a few years. I don't do that anymore. In 1982 I learned about Big League Baseball on TV and I've been an Avid Tiger fan ever since. I go to Detroit two or three times a year so see a game. Sometimes I go to Chicago when the Tigers are playing there. And I usually see the rest of the games on TV. I keep score too! I have tons of Baseball paraphernalia. Literally thousands of cards, many of them autographed by players and officials. I have letters from many of them, and I've made photographs of many players at the games I've gone to.

Now tell me, when did I have time to get wrinkles, gray hair and aged? But not to worry. I have since found the time and I think I've done a great job of it.

And in my advancing "age" I have collected some great in-laws. I've loved all of them except one. The Bad Apple! Three of my children are divorced, but I'm not divorced from any of them. They are still my family members. I felt my girls were wrong in the divorces and I still do. I think divorce is a plague in the land just like aids and cancer.

I'm sure my parents did not like my choice of a husband (neither did I in a very short time) and they let me know it, yet they helped us out a few times when they could. Later on there was some jealousy over the grandchildren. We all thought my youngest sister's children got the better part of their time. My sister lived in the house with my folks after her divorce. Now I have a daughter and two small boys living in my house with me and I get the same feedback from my other children. Now I understand the situation a bit better.

I call this part "Words of Wisdom." The Bible says, "Can two walk together, except they be agreed?" (Amos 3:3) So please don't rush into marriage. There is plenty of time. Better to wait and be sure than to spend years in misery because you couldn't wait. One thing I know personally, God will forgive you for anything, even marrying the wrong person. But let me say, that won't keep you from living with the results of your poor decision. And life can last a long time.

Now we leave the marriage counseling and go to music or a reasonable facsimile. I always loved music and tried to play it on anything I could. We always had access to guitars and, once in a while, I got a chance to try to play a piano. After I moved to Holland and got a good job, I bought myself a Lowery "Genie" Organ. I played it, too. In the middle of the day when everyone was gone to work, or the middle of the night when folk were trying to sleep. No, I am not a musician but it doesn't hurt to pretend, does it?

I can't say I have any charities. I've always been the charity. I have donated seven gallons of blood to the Red Cross. I've given to the Cancer Society and liver funds when I can. I also give what I can to Hospice and Paralyzed Vets.

And as for church, I've nearly always been active in church. I used to teach the six-year-olds in Sunday School, but teenagers have always been my first love. As a child we were taught about the Bible—about the outstanding characters in the Bible—my mother taught us about Abraham, Isaac, Jacob, Daniel, Jonah, Noah, and many of the better known men of the Bible. But it was all just head knowledge, no spirit. Then when I was about twenty-three years old, I found Jesus to be a real person and he became the focal point in my life. Throughout the years following that discovery, He has been a faithful friend, never failing me! I wish I could say I'd always been the same.

Now we talk about the great privilege of reading! I have a lot of favorite authors. I guess the Apostle Paul, who wrote most of the New Testament, is my favorite author. But aside from the Bible I have many favorites. May I name a few of them? Edgar Allan Poe, Jack London, Leon Uris, Sydney Sheldon, Terry C. Johnson, Calleen McCollough, Emily Bronte, Elizabeth B. Browning, Marie Carelli, Clay Fisher, and Frank G. Slaughter. A diversified group! And I do, especially love poetry.

I do not know much about immigration. But I do know my father's family has been traced back for six generations. We discovered they came from North Carolina to Tennessee. Then to Illinois and later to Arkansas. They are buried in Illinois and Arkansas. There is an Underwood cemetery in Piggott, Arkansas, owned and maintained by the family. I visited there in 1990 and was totally amazed to find my name on several monuments or headstones. I got the feeling I could just take my choice (when the time comes) and lay down with my ancestors.

On this trip I found a lot of interesting data on my past. For instance, I had five great, great uncles that fought in the Civil War. Four of them fought for the Union and one for the Confederacy. One of these uncles died in Andersonville, Georgia in that infamous prison camp. I know lots of stories about this period of history, but it will have to wait until another time.

We had relatives who fought in the Revolutionary War. Several were in World War 1. I had a cousin who died at Pearl Harbor. My brother fought for four years in the South Pacific. Some fought in Korea, Vietnam and Somalia. I guess you might say we're a fighting bunch of people!

I remember the Great Depression and Prohibition. I've lived through several wars. I know about tornadoes, floods and droughts. I guess you could say I know a lot of stuff about stuff.

I graduated 8th grade in 1936.

I got my G.E.D. certificate in 1975.

I got a real diploma from 12th grade 1978.

I received a walnut and bronze plaque that says:

Fay Imogene Key
"Highest Grade Point Average"
Adult Highschool Completion
Class of 1978
Community Education
Holland - West Ottawa - Saugatuck
Public Schools

So ask me, am I proud, and I'll say, yeah! For there was a time, back in 1936, when it seemed totally impossible.

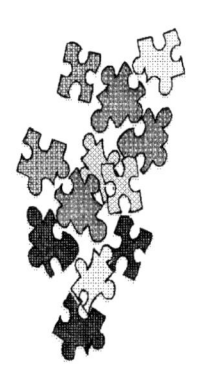

For the Good Times, Some of the Time!

I believe Stewart Hamblin wrote the song, "The love of God." And it says something like this, "Could we with ink the ocean fill, and were the skies with parchment made. Were every stalk on earth a quill and every man a scribe by trade...." This verse says so much to me. There are so many words and so many combinations of words. So many ways to say what needs to be said. And I do need to say a lot of things!

I have some stories (some documents) about my relatives who fought in the Civil War. I'd love to write some of these at a later date, but right now there are things that need to be said that seem more important. For I do find my priorities change from time to time.

Now for longstanding friendships! I have not kept in touch with many from my childhood. I was very shy and backward and didn't make a lot of close friends. So my long-term friendships go back to the year I moved to Michigan in 1952.

I remember a very special friend named Grace Hiatt in South Haven, who was everything to me that a Christian should be. She and I had a Christian bond between us that I don't believe could ever be broken.

The one thing that stands out in my memory is from the year of 1956. My four small children were nine, seven, three and a half, and one year old at the time, and they all came down with the measles. That bad variety! They were so very ill. They had high temperatures, nosebleeds, vomiting and some other conditions that I'll not get into. My husband worked at a shop in South Haven where we lived at the time. When he came home from work he demanded his sleeping time. He was funny about time! He had to have time to be young and free. He had to be able to go to the bars and drink and chase the women. And as for me, I knew something about time also. In my time I had the full care and responsibility of seven children. Well, that was my job, wasn't it?

So with the help of the Lord and my dear friend Grace, we managed to get through this difficult time. And we all made it and we are alive today, except the father!

Grace would come in and sort of take over for a while and insist that I lie down for a while to rest. Of course, I couldn't stay down for the constant needs of the children. It was a little easier just knowing someone cared. Just asking for a drink of water would bring on a nosebleed, and the nosebleed would trigger the vomiting. Grace would go from washing sick little faces to scrubbing solid wooden floors to washing dirty clothes in a zinc tub with a scrub board.

Jesus said no greater love existed than for a man to lay down his life for a friend. Grace gave us her life for many days at a time. And this is just one episode in our life and of our friendship. She also fed us when we were hungry. She gave her whole self and I will always hold this woman in the highest esteem. I thank God for her always. She wanted no credit for what she did. In fact, she said she didn't remember the incident when I mentioned it one time years later. Isn't that just like a Christian? But I'm sure God remembers, and I certainly remember. She was my best friend until her death last summer. I gave the eulogy at her funeral.

I've always had good health. My children are now grown up and in good health. But I sometimes feel a need to remind them there are a lot of serious diseases out there. In fact, every one of my father's family have died from cancer. My mother's family all died from high blood pressure and strokes. And there's aides and many sexually transmitted diseases. So we have to protect ourselves from any of them that we can. Eating right and exercising can help. Trusting God helps too.

I recall a lot of surgeries in my life, but not a lot of sickness. Several years ago I picked blueberries all day. When I got home the pain started and by midnight, when my husband got home from work, I had to be taken the hospital. At 8 a.m. the next day my appendix had to be removed. I was home three days later taking care of my children and helping take care of my brother's family who were with us for a few weeks. This was about 1964.

Then in 1973 a similar thing occurred. My gallbladder went goofy. Same story. Not sick, just a bunch of pain. Then in 1980 I had my tonsils out. Yes, I said my tonsils. I was only fifty-nine years old.

Then within the last few years, I've fallen upstairs and tripped over a small piece of carpet and fell into my bathroom, head first. They both resulted in shoulder surgery. A doctor put me back together and I soon felt fine, again. But when I found my arm wouldn't work right, I went back to the hospital and had surgery for a torn rotator cuff. It healed up in no time and I was fine again. Never any lingering problems.

The surgeon who fixed my arm, Dr. Rhind, is the person who encouraged me to write. He saw early on that I had a lot to say and no difficulty saying it. So he said I should write. He may have created a monster!

And now my formula for healthy living! That's easy. "Eat whatever is set before you and give thanks for it." Eat more fruit and veggies.

As I look back now, for a while, at my parents, I find that I have become what I never thought I would become. After trying hard not to do this, I see things much the way my folks saw them. My mother was the disciplinarian, so we got mad at her a lot. Dad was adored for the opposite side of the same coin. Not much discipline! But someone had to do it. Thank God, somebody cared what we did.

Now let's talk about home remedies. That's a good one. We doted on these three:

#1. If you cut your hand or foot, you soaked it in a pan of kerosene.

#2. If you had chills and fevers, you were given Nash's chill tonic. It was horrendous! A vile tasting liquid with little hard white balls of quinine floating in it. Vick's Vaporub was generously applied to your chest, neck and under your nose, if you had a cold.

#3. And if you needed help with your elimination process, you were given Black Draught made into a tea. Another foul-smelling mess.

I told this to a doctor in South Haven, and he said, "And you lived in spite of it." It was crude and primitive but it worked.

And now, to talk about presidents! We older, poor people adored F. D. Roosevelt. We could begin to see some changes in our lives. We ate better. We had mattresses to sleep on rather than making a large (we called it a bed tic) and stuffing it full of corn shucks for a mattress. The changes came slowly but we could see change.

Then we tried to love Richard Nixon for he was my mother's distant cousin. We did love Eisenhower, because he was a great war hero. I personally loved Jimmy Carter, because I believe him to be an honorable and morally upright man. A Christian man, I believe. A man of integrity. I voted for Clinton because he represented change and again, we needed it badly. I did not believe he was God, and sure enough, he's not. He disappointed me badly. But he's not the first man in high office to sin. They have been doing it for centuries. It's too bad because they wear a very heavy mantle. We look up to them for guidance and feel betrayed when they fail. In the first place, we ought to be putting our utmost trust in God, who never fails anyone. And after all the scandal, I still think he could've made a difference had we been faithful to hold him up in prayer.

More questions—more answers. Yes, I've been widowed. I'm sure I've written about that part of my life in another segment of this story. I did not feel like a fifth wheel. I didn't have time for a lot of negativity. I was too numb, at first. But later, when I did remarry, and it was such a farce of a marriage, I wished I had remained numb, if you get my drift!

Now to talk about wars. I've lived through a few. World War II was the very worst one in my opinion. Every young male in my world went to war. But the worst part was when my eighteen-year-old brother went. After Pearl Harbor was bombed on December 7, 1941, every battle we fought was lost for the first two years. We had no battleships left. And whoever heard of a war being fought on the sea, but with battleships?

There were some ships left after the initial strike at Pearl Harbor, but they were not battleships. It took two years to build a battleship, so the war went very badly for two years. When my brother and thousands of other young men sailed out from San Diego, California, their orders were, "Find the enemy, engage him in battle and hold them at bay as long as you can!" No help or assistance was promised in the near future. Help did come, later, and everyone living today knows the outcome of that war.

Another war seems less likely now, than it has in a long time, so people are able to think of things they would like to do. Personally, I long to visit the Vietnam Monument in Washington. Why that one, I'm not sure.

And now for technological changes, and there have been multitudes of them. My dad used a carbide lamp to hunt with. It was attached to his hunting cap so he could see in the woods after dark. In our homes we used kerosene lamps to light our way. Every afternoon, late, it was someone's job to clean the blackened chimneys for the lamps. Most homes had at least two or three lamps. We had one. No big job! I remember seeing my first gas light. They were in a church. Then they began to show up in other community buildings and later, in homes. We never had one. Guess why!

Of course, electricity followed soon. Then came telephones, all kinds of appliances, all the great things that make our lives so much easier. 'Bout time, I say!

I remember going to a neighbor's house to listen to a big-time boxing match on a radio in 1930. I heard these voices, didn't know where they were coming from or how they got in the little brown box. It was Max Baer or Max Schmelling, I think. I know it was before Joe Louis.

I don't remember when I saw my first TV. I do remember the first one I ever owned. It was in 1968. It was black and white. It cost $20.00. My kids really did love this TV.

Yes, I've seen many changes in my lifetime, and they have not all been good. But a good share of them probably were. I surely wouldn't want to give up my refrigerator, freezer, lights, waterbed or my car. I do like some of the changes.

Now, for music and that's a good one! I remember walking to my dad's house to listen to the Grand Ole Opery on the radio on Saturday nights. My dad and I loved Red Skelton. He could be real funny without getting vulgar. He was COOL! It was all I had access to at the time and it was good.

Now we've passed Grand Ole Opery and get into Rock and Roll. Man, that was a trip! My teenagers made sure I heard plenty of that. As time passed I came to accept it as part of my life. I didn't have to like or dislike it. But since I love music, it wasn't all bad. It was a learning experience. I even went to the Silver Dome once to see Simon and Garfunkle. I liked them "real good." Still do, but don't tell anyone. I also went to Pine Knob to see Bob Seager. I loved him too, at one time.

My folks did the best they could with what they had to do with. I have no feelings of resentment, longings or disappointments. They did their best, and that's all a person can do. I've done the same, for mine, and I feel no shame. One's best ought to be good enough, don't you think?

As for holidays, we didn't do much celebrating. We, as children, didn't know what celebrate meant. We did get a gift for Christmas. It wasn't a big thing, but we loved and took care of it. We always got an apple, an orange, a handful of nuts and some candy. That was standard fare. We could count on that. We were happy with it, and it was a long time between Christmasses.

I retired in July of 1984. I felt I could no longer do enough work for the amount of money I was being paid. My right shoulder had arthritis in it and it was getting harder to keep up my part of the job. So I retired at sixty-three years of age. I made no plans for retirement. I just quit! Then I had a rude awakening. Where was the money coming from? But I made the proper adjustments and I've done fine!

And in my lifetime I've seen and remember many things. The Great Depression, the fall of the Berlin Wall. I saw the Soviet Union fall apart. I saw the first capsule go up into space and then come down in the ocean. I saw the Challenger blow up in the air after only a few seconds from launch, killing all aboard. I've seen many things both good and bad. I saw a president gunned down in the streets of Dallas. I've seen soldiers and sailors march proudly away and never return. And through all of it, I've seen God's hand available to help any who would call on Him. I saw a terrible drought in 1930 and I've seen it rain on the just and on the unjust. Isn't God wonderful?

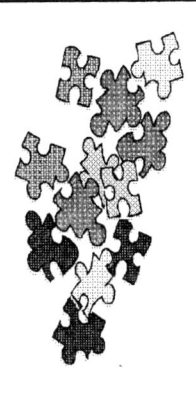

Good Bye Jon-Jon

For very obvious reasons known to all America, I've been drawn this week to a particular person, family and set of events (past and present). And as I am somewhat a history buff and an avid collector of news, I've ingested a lot of news and pictures in the last week. It's been very sad, to say the least. I've felt a lot of grief for the family members and for America as a whole.

I don't deny my heartache! I don't deny the sadness I feel! Now I know that with God one soul is the same as another soul, but in America, this boy was special! We all knew him, in our own way. He was our little boy!

So much was expected of him. He lived with a lot of pressure. I thought he handled it quite well, generally. Very rarely did he let his feelings show. It appeared to show only when his wife or a close friend felt threatened by reporters.

With all the money and means at his disposal, he could have had or indulged in all kinds of excesses. His outward looks showed he was not a drunk or a gluttonous man. It seems he will be remembered not as a great man, but as a good man. Had he lived out a normal lifetime, the greatness was probably just around the next corner!

Not just because of his looks, even though he was a simply beautiful human being, he will be remembered as a perfect gentleman.

It seems he was larger than life, even in death. But in spite of all the affluence we may or may not enjoy in this life, there is a greater factor to consider. And that is the individual's relationship with the Creator. So, as far as the Kennedy's are concerned, my simple prayer is that in what is presumed to be an out of control, death-spiraling of the plane, they had the ability to call on God! For we are taught, "if we call upon God, He'll hear and save". Psalms 86:5 and Joel 2:32 are two good examples of this.

So, through all of my personal pain and through my many tears, I found one thought coming through clearly above all else.

"Oh God, that all America would be drawn to you, even as they have been drawn to this tragedy!"

A True Story about My Eldest Son

I think I'll call this another chapter in the continuing saga of the Key family history. A visit from my son recently brought some of it to my attention, but some of it I have known for a very long time.

My son's name is Roy F. Key Jr. He came to me with a story I want to repeat, but I'll have to go back to the beginning to set this story up properly and to explain some of his behavior. I'll have to explain his birth somewhat. I'm not a medical person. I don't know if my theory is right or not, but I truly believe his birth conditions had something to do with his mental attitude in later years.

On Monday morning, May 12, at six a.m. I started labor for his birth. Finally on Friday, May 16, at 11:05 he was pulled from my body with forceps. He was a badly beaten little kid, but seemed okay otherwise. In three months he was the most beautiful little boy with a great personality, friendly and lovable. Everyone loved him and especially his mom.

The change came gradually. I can't remember a time and put a finger on it, but a change did come! We used to say he had a quick temper. But now that I look back, it was more like a rage that came over him from out of nowhere, and he would not seem to know what he was doing. He fought a lot growing up. He would strike out at the least or no cause. A psychologist told his wife he had acute paranoia. He always thinks people are out to get him or to do him wrong. No one will give him a chance. They won't pay him for the work he does. They won't let him make a living. He is a very good auto mechanic. So what gives? Do we have a modern day Jeckyl and Hyde? But here is the other side, and this is my story. Animals love him. He has a way with them.

Now we have a completely different kind of person, a happier kid, with so much love and concern for helpless little things. So now, I am ready to tell the story!

Several years ago he found a baby raccoon on the side of the road. He immediately stopped to get it and took it home. He fed and nurtured it, and it grew up in his house and yard. It would come to the door and scratch to get in. He and his wife named this little kid, Bud. We have enlarged pictures of Bud in our picture albums. This kid had the best of two worlds. We heard a lot about Bud over the phone, the changes Bud went through, the cute things he did, and so forth.

Then one day my son, my very temperamental son, called and (almost in tears) said, "Mom, Bud didn't come home last night."

I tried to console him by explaining that Bud was almost an adult and had probably gone off to find someone who spoke his language.

Well, in time, Bud came back, and Roy called me again overjoyed. We all rejoiced with him, and then Bud disappeared again. By now we had gotten used to the idea of Bud's leaving for good. Several weeks or even months passed, and we thought the coon chapter was closed. It had been a great experience and a joy to have aided and abetted this guy in the growing up process in an alien concept.

Some time later, my son was awakened one night by his dogs barking like crazy. When they wouldn't shut up, he took his flashlight and went out to investigate. Just outside his backdoor, he has this bird feeder high up on a pole. So as he shined his light up this pole, he is delighted to see five pairs of shiny eyes looking back at him. Bud had come home with four babies. Roy helped her provide for this new family until they were grown, and one day, they all left again. Some time later, Bud came back and Roy helped her raise the second family. She must have trusted Roy to allow him to participate in raising two families. We still mention Bud with affection on occasion.

Roy and Bud

Bud

A baby deer that Roy raised

To Advertise or Not

Some people get their inspiration to write in the strangest places. For instance, this morning as I was returning from my garden, I saw a simple sight that set my mind to working overtime. I trust God had something to do with this since all of my life seems to be a tug of war between my new spiritual man being pitted against the old fleshly man, who by the way is supposed to be dead.

As I drove down the street today I saw a simple sight. A Pepsi Cola truck was being unloaded by a regular-looking man in regular work clothes. But something caught my eye. He had a wide, black elastic band fastened around his waist. Nothing too unusual about this as lots of people wear tight elastic bands around their waists to indicate a weak or injured back. But here's where my mind got squirrelly. I started thinking back through my life and some other scenes came to mind. They are all about people I know or have known. No names, of course!

First of all, I remember several times, in my fifteen years at General Electric when I went to a chiropractor for back problems. And I often wore a wide band of elastic around my waist or lower back. Or maybe I did play up or give in to my condition somewhat. "I don't think I can help move that chair," or whatever the situation called for. Please don't take this wrong. My back was always weak even when I was a small child. Honest! But these treatments felt so good, and after all, I did need a few days off from work for this to heal. My insurance company was paying hundreds of dollars for my T. L. C., and I didn't want to re-injure myself while I was getting better. So please don't ask me to do anything! See where I'm going?

Here's another case. My sister who visits me occasionally never fails to get my attention this way. When she gets up to go anywhere, kitchen, bathroom or whatever, here's the routine. She always staggers a little, grabs for a chair or the wall, clutches her heart with the other hand and leaning on the closest prop she pants, puffs and huffs, or whatever the occasion calls for, and after a short pause, goes blithely on her way. This sign is as obvious as the elastic band. She has let me know she is a needy person. Okay! I get it!

Case number three: A person playing for sympathy in another manner. They will make a terrible-looking mug from a normal-looking face and make a statement something like this. "I've had this awful headache for a week. I'll bet I've taken a whole bottle of aspirin and it just don't get better. I don't know what I'm gonna do. I've got all these things I need to get done, and I just don't feel like doing anything." Her answer comes when another person speaks up and says, "Honey, you go lie down and I'll put a cool cloth on your head. I'll watch the children for a while. After all, I've got a couple of hours before I have to be at home. And, Dear, where is your mop? I'll clean up this floor while you get a nap." Mission accomplished! It worked, didn't it?

And case number four: Two people broke their ankles at the same time. They do have different kinds of jobs and different circumstances, but watch. In two or three days one of them is back to work, doing his normal job, walking up and down stairs. The other man cries a lot! His pain is unbearable. He's always wondering, why me? And when he finally gets back in church, he carries this big, ugly, gnarly stick for a crutch! This tells his friends he's crippled. This is his elastic band, attention-getter! I guess we all have our own badges we wear to our best advantage.

But there is another side to this coin. And it is this. In the spiritual world, if we have a head problem we are instructed to put on the helmet of salvation, to put away evil from our lives, to get rid of ugly black cancer giving thoughts, depart from sin, begin to think the thoughts of Christ. Now, we don't have to put on a mug that is self-made, which is a badge of sorts, also. Is that possible, you ask? Oh, yes! Not always easy, but absolutely possible.

Now to follow on through. If we feel weak, what can we do? Do we go for the elastic band? I think not, but rather choose to be strengthened with might in our inner man. So we gird up our lower back with the truth of God's word. Then we become strong in the power of His might!

And if our heart is our problem? God said he would give us a fleshly heart for our heart of stone. A heart that will love Him and seek after Him. A heart that desires to do His bidding. Now we have it all.

How about your feet or ankles? Do you have a problem in this area? Do your feet seek the wrong paths? I've got that answer, too. God says we are to have our feet shod with the preparation of the Gospel of peace. Okay? No more roaming in dangerous paths. No more endless endangerment to your whole being through your feet. The path is now straight.

Now since these helps from God are invisible, we might as well add the breastplate of righteousness and the shield of faith and be protected against all evil. These are not outward badges, but protection anyway!

Now it's time to choose your armor. Will you continue to wear badges, get as much pity as you can, alibi your weaknesses? Or will you ask God to change your entire thinking, start to walk upright and be strong in Him? Which will it be?

Looking Back, But Pressing Ahead

I was sitting in a waiting room in a hospital Monday, August 23, 1999, reading an article by Tom Brokaw. He wrote about growing up on a farm in South Dakota. I think he basically wrote about his father's work ethics and about the Great Depression and was speaking of his book, *The Greatest Generation*. I loved his book. I love Tom Brokaw! Period!

While reading his article I discovered I'd like to write my memories of the depression years and the way we worked. I don't know if anyone is interested in this, or not, but I **need** to write it down. So here goes.

I do not write this to cause shame to my memory of my parents. They did the very best they could with what they had to do work with, and in the part of the country we lived in.

I was born in the southeastern part of Missouri, very near the Arkansas line, in 1921. By the time I can remember, we had moved to northeastern Arkansas. This was in 1924 or 1925. I can look back and remember where we lived every year. That's how I keep track of things. We lived in the cotton growing area of the United States. I never knew why we moved every year, but I suppose my father thought he would get a better deal, would come out with more money at the end of the year, or reap some financial benefit from the move. But we didn't! Things never changed! Only the houses changed, and mostly for the worse. When I look back, I can't believe some of the shacks we lived in. We didn't think much of it at the time, for we'd never had anything else to compare our lives to. My mother must have hated our lifestyle. Our dad never complained. He must have had a great tolerance for things he had no power to change.

The work situation was simple. You could work by the day, sharecrop, or rent. Renting meant you owned your own livestock and tools and could buy your own feed and seed for planting. That sort of thing. We never rented!

When you worked by the day, you went where your boss sent you and did whatever he told you to do. You were paid by the week. I do not know what my dad made in a week. I wish I knew, but you wouldn't believe it anyway.

This went on until about 1934, when we graduated to sharecropping. I do remember that we lived better from 1929 through 1933. We had better houses anyway. I very distinctly remember my father coming home, I believe it was October 29, and announcing to my mom that all the banks had busted! It didn't mean a lot to me, as I'd never been in a bank, had no interest in or connection to a bank. It was all Greek to me. But I did get this one picture in my head of dollar bills exploding up and out of the top of a building and then starting to float down on the breezes. You know something? I never did find one of those paper dollars, and I did look! I was not yet eight years old.

By 1934 we are sharecroppers and back to really bad houses again. Today I look back to the years '29 through '33 as the best part of growing up, even though a baby brother was born and died in these years. I was too young to understand it at the time. I grieved later for him.

One thing I remember is the big gardens we always had. We looked forward to the time when the young onions and lettuce was big so we could start eating it. We usually had some chickens, so we had eggs part of the time. My mom would collect eggs till there were about sixteen and then a mother hen would sit on them and hatch baby chicks. And then in a few weeks we could have fried chicken. Mama had to fib to us and say the horses stepped on them. Boy, how I wish fried chicken still tasted as good as it did then!

I can't remember ever being hungry, but we sure did get tired of beans and potatoes. During these good years we got a cow. I don't know how. We kept her for a very long time. She was like part of the family. I don't remember her after 1937.

I know we usually had one big hog that Dad fattened up for winter. So part of the time we had pork in some form, till it was gone. This was before pressure cookers, so this meat was cured by packing it in salt. We ate it as fast as we could, so it wouldn't spoil.

My dad dug holes in the ground, lined the hole with dry straw, and in it he stored sweet and Irish potatoes for the winter. Mom canned tomatoes, pickles and all the vegetables she could for the winter also. We grew a lot of our food. We picked and shelled great northern and pinto beans and stored them also for winter. We treated them for weevils, but it didn't always work!

So when the cow went dry, the hens didn't lay eggs, the salt pork was gone, in short, when all else failed, we went back to dried beans and potatoes. For breakfast we could most always depend on oatmeal, gravy and homemade biscuits. Mom and Dad had coffee.

Once or twice I remember Dad buying a gallon bucket of Sorghum molasses. What a neat change! It was sweet so it was good.

1935 was a tough year. I remember my dad walking three miles, hitching up the mules and plowing all day long for someone, and then walking all the way back home. And he had earned 75 cents for a day, not an hour. Hard to believe, isn't it?

1936 was much better. Things were better with the government too. The Great Depression was dying. We made a good crop. We even had money when the year was over, so we bought new (cheap) mattresses, new coats for Mom and I, and a lot of groceries to keep us fed through the winter.

Early in 1937 we had a great flood and the muddy water stood four feet deep in our house. We had to move out for several days, and there went our mattresses, coats and everything we owned. Everything! That included family pictures, birth records and keepsakes—everything!

Now we are back to working for another farmer. But not to worry. There is a war brewing over in Europe and beginning to threaten us. With war comes a lot of death and destruction. But the financial status usually gets a boost, and there's more money to be had by all. Let me say here, I think war is too high a price to pay for a little prosperity.

But things in general are better. People are forgetting the depression, but it's too late for some people to ever enjoy good times. My father died in 1970 without ever having owned a home, and not because he wasn't a hard worker. It just came too late in his life. The good times, I mean. I'd hate to see someone today, asked to do the kind of work my dad had to do.

I am seventy-eight years old. I've lived here for thirty years. I paid for my house a long time ago and I love and enjoy it. But I've always felt a little guilty because my parents never owned a home.

I do thank God for the good times and I also thank Him for my memories of the bad times, which really weren't too bad, after all.

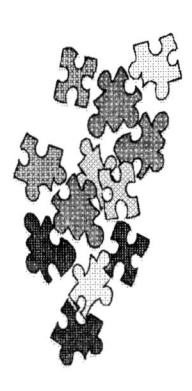

Tearing Down the Barn

And just when I thought it couldn't get any worse, would you believe it did? Did you ever hear a tale like that before? But I'm getting ahead of myself. So back to the beginning! I've lived in this house for twenty-seven years. I've also paid insurance on it for twenty-seven years. Several years ago my garage began to look kind of sickly. Well, it never occurred to me that I ought to do something about it. I guess I thought it would last forever, like I plan to do. Well guess what?—the barn didn't make it! For the last several years I've been hoping it would just fall down. Then I could collect my insurance and build a new one. That's what insurance is for, isn't it? Surprise, surprise! It didn't work that way.

A couple of years ago I called my insurance company and told them about the situation, and asked if I would be allowed to take it down before it fell on my neighbor's building. "Oh, no!" they say, "it must be an act of God."

So I explain to them, as clearly as I can, that I don't believe God is in the barn wrecking business. Well, they won anyway! Then on the tenth of June, I was given a limited time to get the barn down or be fined. Now I didn't think that was very nice. But it surely did open my eyes, and I started to make plans. That's when things got tough, if you know what I mean!

I have a standing date with my son to have breakfast with him every Saturday morning, so on June 21, as we were eating, I told him of my situation. He said, "We can do that. No problem!" And I thought, this is going to be easy. Another young man spoke up and said he knew where he could dump the trash for free. I thought, wow! This is going to be a breeze. So my daughter, Melodi, and I set about getting a trailer to haul the junk on. She knows some people and got the trailer. But then remembered that none of us can back a rig of this size down my drive—I mean, the ones of the family that were available at the time! You see, everyone in my family works at different jobs and at different times. I don't always have a driver with a class two C.D.I. operator's license just standing by waiting for my command, "Men, start your engines."

Now for the next problem. The trailer has a fine hitch on it, but the truck does not have a ball on it. So we go to my son's place of work, and he proceeds to torch the hole in the truck to fit the ball we had borrowed. This turns out to be much harder than we had expected. But we finally got it fixed, then borrowed a driver to back the rig into my drive and park the truck and trailer. And now we can start the job! And boy oh boy what a job!

Now for the actual work of putting the lumber on the trailer. It was not as hard as some of the other things we had to do. Then for lack of a driver, the loaded trailer remained parked in my drive for several days. When finally we got things together off we went to the dump. And I, being the privileged character that I am, sat in the truck while the other five people unloaded the trailer. Sounds easy, don't it? Well, it's not. But they got it all unloaded, and we got back home.

Now that should be the end of the story, don't you think? But nooooo! We parked the trailer and could not get the ball and hitch separated. We tried everything we could think of, but to no avail. We finally got a neighbor to come over and help us. He knew about farm tools, but it still took him a very long time to separate the hitch and the ball.

My daughter helped by making lemonade. It was really hot! It took so long and it was so hot! I couldn't believe all the trouble. The mental part was the worst part of the whole job.

Well, all of that happened on Saturday, Monday, Tuesday and Wednesday. And here it is Friday, the end of the week, and everybody's got things to do. Most of them are going to a concert tonight. Mel's family is going on vacation, after the concert, and she will not leave until the last load of lumber has been hauled away. That means another hard day of loading and hauling trash. So that's what we did on Friday. It was a long hot day, everyone was beat, and ahead lay the concert and a long trip to Iowa.

Mel would not put off the trash hauling till next week, and Ken would not put off the trip until Saturday morning! So off they went! I guess all's well that ends well. That's what I've heard. Mel called me about noon on Saturday. They had a great trip. They went through Wisconsin, Minnesota, South Dakota, and then down to Iowa.

Now it's Sunday, June 29th. The garage is gone, the family is gone, I'm alone, Mel's car won't start, and I missed church. How's that for the luck of the Irish? Something here does not seem kosher!

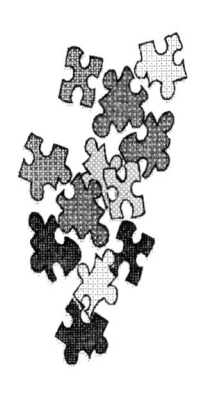

Dual Personality

From the start I want to say that I DO NOT believe in these overrated movies about people who don't know who they are! Maybe today I am Emile, yesterday I was Ruth, tomorrow I may be Jane or Evangeline. No, I don't believe in this. I've been ME for seventy-five years. No change for me until the time when I'll be changed in the twinkling of an eye. But until then, I'll just be me.

But then, why the question? I guess it was prompted by some of the foolishness that's on the TV. Is God a man or a woman? I don't spend my days in front of the tube, but I DO like to see the news. I really don't know why, for it's almost always "bad." But it may be a fear of being asked a question about something recent, and not knowing anything about what's going on in the world—a fear of being thought of as dumb or stupid. Which I ain't, and my use of the English language proves that point.

I do have a problem though. You see, I have this boisterous or rambunctious nature; and coupled with the idea that I know something about everything, I've been known to get my foot in my mouth, if you know what I mean. In a regular conversation with people, even important people, I find myself answering before the question has been finished. I don't stop and think of how I'll answer, I just answer. I know how I feel about most things without a moment's hesitation.

I remember embarrassing myself terribly in speaking to a visiting minister once and, of course, I apologized over and over. But it gave me a chance to check myself on my rapid-fire answers to everything. It gave me a chance to notice the dual personality in myself, that I don't believe in!

You see, above every desire in my life, I want to walk and live like a Christian. It's easy to say you're a Christian, but the world wants to see if you ACT like one. So I find myself being torn between my two natures. I have a deep, deep desire to ever be pleasing to the Lord, and yet, I have this goofiness or slightly comedic way of addressing things. I tell myself that laughter doeth good like a medicine. It's okay not to be terribly serious all the time.

But after life has buffeted me around for a while, I sometimes feel a need to slow down, commune with my spirit and touch God for my needs. It is then that I have to go to that quiet and secret place within me where my family and friends cannot go. They've never been invited there! It's a place that only the Lord knows about. And knowing that He's always welcome, He meets me there and we commune. In the stillness within me, when I've brought my spirit into subjection, I find the peace and fulfillment I need, nay, must have. It's a fuel station. Then I come out to the real world again, and I'm immediately met with diverse problems. And with seven children, there's always problems. I seem to always have answers to their questions. Isn't that wonderful?

Now for the finale:

When my children were young I had them in church every time I could get there. I often had to bum rides! So I know they have a strong base to build on. But until they are ready to make the firm commitment to the Lord, I want to be able to stand in the gap and make up the hedge in their behalf.

I have no doubt they will come in "someday," but I often find myself wishing I could know "when." But I guess that's what faith is for, huh? No comedic answers. No dual thoughts. Just one desire.

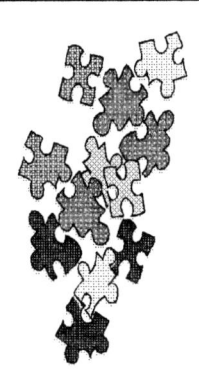

Rockyfellow Plaza

This week, watching "The Today Show" on NBC, I saw a scene that brought back a memory to me of my first time in the Plaza, several years ago. You notice I said, "first time," as if I'd been there many times. Well, I have been there twice, possibly three times. Now I know that doesn't make me a world traveler, but I do pay close attention when I go to new places. I'm very curious. I want to know everything about everything.

So I start looking into the history pertaining to this place. I do serious research on things that no one else would care about. I had to find out which one of the Titan Gods was on the west wall of the ice rink, just under the Christmas tree that goes up every year in the Plaza. I found out that it was Prometheus. Then I also found out that he was the firstborn of twins. His name, meaning forethought, shows that he was expected, planned on and looked for. On the other hand, his brother, Epimetheus, which means afterthought, was a surprise as his name indicates.

Then I checked further and found the name of the model who posed for the making of the statue. The statue weighs nine tons. The model died in 1998. Isn't that interesting? You needed to know that, didn't you? I also found that Prometheus, supposedly, gave us fire. Now that's nice to know, too. And where am I going with all of this, you may ask? And I would truthfully acknowledge, I really don't know.

But back to the memory that came to me. It was my second trip to New York and my son-in-law was showing us (my daughter and me) the city. We were sightseeing big time. And then we missed the last ferry going over to Ellis Island. And that really hurt, for I know that the ancestors of all of us came through that place to get to where we are now. I really wanted to see that. But John took me to see a Yankee ballgame later that day, and that helped ease my pain a little bit.

But back to the ice rink again. I don't know how to describe it exactly, but it was like a very large basement with the house removed from off it. You are walking down the street where the General Electric building is found. The NBC studios are all inside, and you are at ground level. Then you take a lone flight of stairs down and find yourself in a very grand restaurant (if it is summer), or an ice rink (if it is winter).

So here we go down the stairs, and I'm trying to pretend I know what I'm doing. Imagine this! I'm past sixty years old. I'm overweight, seriously, and dressed in my very best mid-western garb that didn't look too badly when I was in Holland, Michigan. But now I'm rubbing elbows with models, movie stars, Broadway people and the like; and I'm suddenly self-conscious about who I am and how I look. And the funny thing is no one knows I'm there, except my family. But I guess this is a woman thing, thinking about how I look.

And I am so concerned that I don't look like I fit in, so I need to act in such a way that no one will know I don't! Now to whom do we credit this? It sounds a little like pride, doesn't it? But let me assure you it is not entirely attributed to pride. I have always had this need to know stuff! Not to impress anyone, I can't do that very effectively, but I just need to know. You might call it a craving to know. I was labeled a child with a great curiosity.

As I grew up and grew older, I was consumed with my family's welfare and other related things. And then one day my kids were grown up and gone, and I had nothing to do. So I'm back to my original questions, like: Why? How come? And what for?

So I read the dictionary and the World Book Encyclopedia. Is that weird, or what? If you need to know something, just ask me, and I'll try to find someone who can answer your question!

Why I am like I am—I remember my father often saying, "A person could be without formal education, but still learn accidentally some things about life, if he was interested. On the other hand, a person could have the greatest education possible and still be ignorant!" And I sort of believe that.

And I ain't ignorant. My use of the English language should prove that!

This Will Be a Quiet Day

I sit here at my table in the cool, quiet stillness of the day, before people and things start with their noises. And I just enjoy the elements this day is made up of. There is a subtle presence I am aware of, and it's great! Psalm 46:10 says, "Be still, and know that I am God." And I believe that's what is happening.

There is one sound coming in from outside. It sounds like a bird feeding her brood.

My grandson's Pomeranian comes down the stairs, toenails clicking. And from the upper floor I hear the fans whirring in the bedrooms. Other than this, all is quiet and peaceful. It is so good to be at peace with all things, feeling secure in my hope for the future.

Not having any jobs that have to be done immediately today, my only chore is to pray for Honduras and our people who are down there ministering to our brothers in and around La Ceiba. I'll probably never get to go to Honduras, but I try to imagine what it is like. Not like Holland, Michigan, I'm sure! It must be very hot, tropical, very verdant and very beautiful, and nonetheless, a third world country. They lack many things we take for granted.

We send them some financial help, our people go there often and help them with building and such, but what we supply them with in abundance is our love and prayers. We have been welded to them in the Spirit. We have become a brotherhood through love in Christ! So we, here at home, await the return of our missionaries and the good report of what God is doing in Honduras. We know it will be good, for when one plants and another waters, then God gives the harvest. We are trusting Him for this. It's His word!

Another thing that makes this day seem so different is the fact that I've been so busy all summer long. I can't remember when I've had so many things to do and all at once! It seems as if everything there is to do has been done (or at least started) this year.

After tearing down the garage, we had to rebuild the dog pen, for the garage provided two sides of the dog pen. After tearing down the building, we had to get it removed from my place. That became a Herculean task. I can't remember ever having worked so hard. Maybe it just takes longer to do a job as you get older.

I'm now waiting to get a new cement driveway built and a utility barn erected. It seems like a never-ending procession of jobs to be done. I have to wait for my help to become available before every job, as it is all volunteer help. It's all free and it's all family. I guess I should not complain about waiting.

So, in light of all that's been done and all that remains to be done, I'm very grateful for the fact that there's absolutely nothing on my agenda today, except my commitment to fast and pray for Honduras. I guess the bottom line is this: If you want your life to run smoothly and with the utmost efficiency, just trust it to the Master Builder. He'll set your days in order and direct your feet in the right path.

Putting aside all things that come to mind that should be done, I quietly rest in the Lord and wait on Him. I just know this is going to be a great day. And it's all mine!

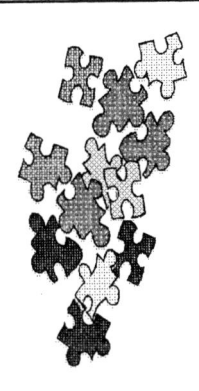

The Rush and Hustle of Christmas

Well, it's finally over, and I can't say I'm sorry. Maybe now, I'll get some rest. Like many others, I've lived Christmas for the last month, at least! Ever since Thanksgiving, I've been concerned, nearly consumed, with Christmas. How many will be here? What will I cook that will be different? And the big question, who will offer to help do the dishes? You know, the important questions in life!

I guess it went pretty well, considering all things. Now for the clean up. And where am I going to store all this stuff? People really are generous, you know. I suppose I ought to be grateful. Well, I've got an empty room upstairs. I guess I'll put it all up there for the moment, and sort it out later. Maybe when spring gets here. Yes, that's what I'm gonna do!

And so I begin quickly packing and trudging up the stairs. Several trips have to be made. And I find my strength waning and my tolerance growing weak. And I'm getting downright tired of Christmas and all it's extra work and trouble. Needless to say, I'm finally through with packing and trudging and stowing away, and I can get to bed and rest, I hope. Wow, am I beat!

I wonder what it is about Christmas that people will nearly kill themselves over! And as I lay there, at last, reliving all the good and the bad parts of the day and I'm fast drifting off to a much needed sleep, I remember...Maybe I ought to pray or give thanks or something. But I find I'm too tired to concentrate, so I ask God if it's okay to rest tonight and pray later. And since He didn't say "no" I went to sleep.

But somewhere in my overworked body and my overtaxed mind, I had a very restless night. And through it all I began to understand one thing that many of us are guilty of forgetting. It was like a dream and the gist of it was: In my rush and anxiety I had packed and hidden away the Babe of Christmas. I had put away the pre-teenage lad who sat and discussed important matters with the high officials of His day. And if you put these things away, there's really not much room for a young miracle-worker who turns water into wine and feeds thousands of hungry followers and raises folks from the dead. And if these things have been forgotten or stored away, then there is no one to go to the cross for our sins. And we find ourselves lost with no Savior!

Oh, God, what a thought! Please let this be a dream! And in His graciousness He reminds me that it's just the Holy Spirit's way of setting things straight and giving me another chance to put first things first.

How grateful I am for another chance to get it right! For without these first aspects of Christ, there could be no cross, no sacrifice for sin and no hope in this world.

I'm going to try real hard to remember what comes first and where to let the other things come into play. The God of second chances is still faithful!

Slappy: My Pretty Girl

Her name was Slappy.

I called her my pretty girl.

She was the sweetest natured pet I ever had.

She came to my house as a small, fuzzy baby, just weaned!

She wasn't mine at that time, but became mine over a few years time.

No one seemed to love her as I did. My son moved out a few years after he had brought her home, but she didn't move for various reasons.

I had a nice doghouse and pen—he didn't. I had another younger puppy, and I thought it would give Slappy a lot of exercise and help keep her young longer. The young Chow puppy was stolen, I think, and my Slappy was on her own for exercise. I couldn't keep up with her, so she spent most of her time in her pen. One of my granddaughters came and walked her when she was in the area.

As she grew older she ate less. And as I was aging also, I would give her two days' rations at one time. When I fed her last week, Saturday, I went in the pen and brushed her hair, petted her and loved her real good. I guess we were saying goodbye, but I didn't know it at the time.

Sunday morning when I went to the car to go to church I saw her lying out in her pen, but not in the house as you would expect. I didn't go out to the pen, as I had provided her Sunday needs on Saturday. As I was leaving, I thought it looked like she was breathing rather hard. I got in my car with mixed emotions, telling myself I'd check with the vet on Monday. I prayed on my way to church, "Lord, if it's her time to go, don't let her suffer. Please spare her any excess pain." When I got home from church, she was dead.

I don't know if it is right or not to pray for your pets, but a praying person prays about just about everything.

Now I guess it's all over, but the terrific loss I'm feeling and an unutterable sadness. And now I wait for God to help me regain the joy of my salvation, and I know He will.

There must be a lesson here somewhere. I'm trying hard to find it!

The Question

Is all snow the same? Well, it's all white. That much is certain! It's main purpose, I think, is to water the ground. And that occurs after the weather warms up, and the snow melts. No great mystery here. But it's not **why** it comes, but **how** it arrives that makes the difference.

Sometimes it comes down in great big white blobs of wetness that you can almost hear when it reaches the ground, or your windowpane, or your car's windshield. This snowfall is called the "oxen" approach, being diligent and getting the job done.

Then there's the snow that comes down to us on butterfly wings. Soft, ever so softly. Such a peaceful feeling, for me, as if God were hiding all the ugliness in the world, if only for a little while.

And then there's the snow that always seems to come out of the West in a horizontal slant with a stiff wind to accompany it, just to make sure it gets where it's going. Now this is the "Napoleon army" approach. Do not try to interfere! This snow is the serious business type.

And there also is the snow that comes in large "kangaroo leaps." One minute it's here, and the next minute it's gone. What's happening? What's going on? Where did it go? It looked as if it would snow for a week! And then it's gone. But not to worry. Before you can ask yourself three questions, behold, it's back again and on big kangaroo hops again.

Now tell me all snow is the same. I think not! But isn't it all just too lovely for words? I could watch it coming down for hours, regardless of the vehicle it chooses to arrive in!

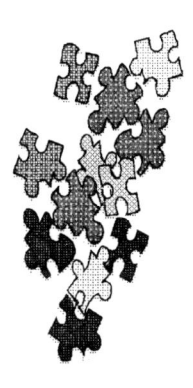

God Help Me Hear Your Voice

Why would a man run from God?
What gives a man the right to believe that he knows more than God?
Can we not learn from other's heartaches?

There are signposts all along the way.
There is no path we can take, but that someone has already been down it.
The signs of shipwreck are everywhere.
Who are we to think we can deviate from God's pattern and find an easier way?
Did not God say, "Here is the way, walk ye in it?"
He did not promise there would always be sunshine, birds singing and flowers blooming.
But He did promise to go with us every step of the way.

Why is it so hard for us to trust Him?
Why do we still feel we can do it our way?
Why would a Christian ever entertain the thought of divorce,
When it goes against everything God's word teaches?
There is a way which seemeth right unto a man, but the end thereof are the ways of death! (Proverbs 14:12)

Why do Christians walk so close to the line?
That divider between right and wrong?
The word tells us to FLEE the very appearance of evil, not to see how close we can get and then jump back at the last minute.
How can we be sure we will be able to jump back in time?

One sad story of a man who thought his way was better than God's way.
You know the story so I'll spare you that much. But can you imagine,
Waking up in a totally black caldron of evil smelling acids, the stench so overpowering you can't open your eyes, you can't get a breath of air.
Sea weeds are wrapped around your head. You are totally powerless to help yourself. You know you can't last very long. Your last thoughts are, "God said, but I did," so in your heart you cry out to God.
And you know what? He heard! He answered! He is good!

But let's learn a lesson here. Let's not abuse our privileges.
Let's not live as sloppily as we can, just because God is good and forgiving.

He just might have a limit! So let's try to walk upright before God and man and do our very best to earn His, "WELL DONE MY GOOD AND FAITHFUL SERVANT!"

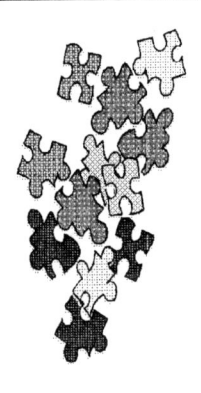

Comparisons

I was thinking how little I give the Lord and how much He gives me. I give Him my heart and a promise to live for Him, and He gives me peace, joy, forgiveness and a promise of a life in Heaven forevermore. I bring Him the ashes of my life, and He gives me beauty. I bring Him my sadness and sorrow, and He gives me gladness, happiness and a reason to live.

I used to spend time thinking of my past and grieving over it. But He said, "Why waste your time with the past? I'm building you a mansion to occupy where you can live and fellowship with me for all of your tomorrows."

Sometimes in my discouragement I say, "Lord, I never seem to do the things I meant to do. I always miss the goals I've set. I guess I am just about worthless."

And He answers, "Anyone that I died to redeem is of great value to me. Do not call what I have cleansed, unclean. As you submit your life to me, I will fashion it into a jewel of great worth. Do not think or speak lightly of what I died for."

So I guess it comes down to purpose and potential!

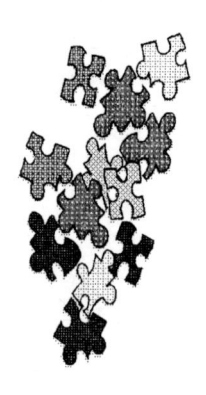

Lord, Help Me

Help me to see with the eyes you gave me.
Help me to hear with the ears I have.
Help me seek and know your will.
Help me follow where you lead.
Help me to be in the place you assigned to me.
Help me to go from following to leading when you
 indicate, and where the need appears.
Help me to be gentle of heart, but strong in spirit.
Help me to be pliable without altering your word.
Help me understand the needs of others and be able to
 help.
Be my strength, Lord, when I am weak.
Be my river in the desert places of my life.
Be my light when the way grows dark.
Be the one constant in my life, the one thing I can
 count on always.
Help me change from passivity to aggressiveness in
 each battle, for we are in a war.
Hold my hand when all others forsake me.
If I falter, be as a magnet that draws me on.
I am a needy person, so Lord, please help me!

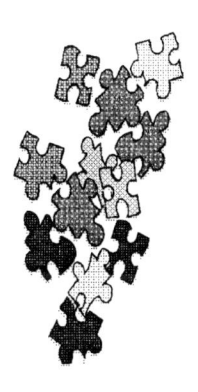

Lord, I Need You!

I feel so inadequate!
Sometimes I need you more than at other times.
I know that in you I live and move and have my being.
I go to the word, Lord, please encourage me.
There is a war going on.
Help me to be a good soldier,
Armed and ready!
When adversity comes, let me be equal to the test.
Make me able to endure!
When my heart is overwhelmed,
As it is today,
Lead me to the rock, wherein I trust.
Let my friends hold my arms up till the storm is past.
Dear Lord, I am so tired.
Help me to rest in you!

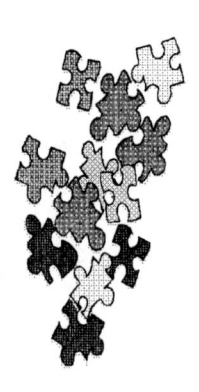

My Request

Be the joy of my life, Lord.
Be the strength in my body.
Be my sunrise every morning.
Be my peace in the nighttime.
Be my hope for my tomorrows.
Be my comfort in all my sorrows.
Be the health and strength in my bones.
Be as a light that emanates from my eyes.
Let the words of my mouth be blessing and instruction
 to others.
Be the first thought I have when I awaken,
And the last thought I have when I retire.
Be the very reason I live,
My all in all,
My everything,
Walk with me, Lord, and talk with me in this life,
And let my entrance into your presence be the
 culmination of all these requests!
Is that asking too much?

Deep Calls to Deep

I'm quick to ask the Lord to help me out,
For headaches or for other aches galore.
I call on Him for each and every thing.
It seems there are more and more and more!

Sometimes I'm asked to write to cheer one up.
And often asked to pray for a friend.
And then a situation shows itself and,
I know the time for playing church must end.

When cancer strikes a person that is dear.
A daughter or a sister, let us say.
And everything within you turns to fear.
You turn to God and don't know what to say.

"I don't know if I'm worthy, Lord, to ask,
I'm such a tiny part of who you are.
It seems such a monumental task,
And Lord, from me to you seems awfully far!"

(continued)

But in my fear I know that I must try.
For in my life right now, there's no way out.
I dig down deep within my heart for faith,
And trust that you will find a good way out.

I labor with my love, my faith, my tears.
I feel so small, but yet, how great my need.
Then I recall I'm yours by covenant,
And I am free to come to you and plead.

When peace begins to flood my soul anew,
I feel I've touched the heart of God again.
It's like He says, "My child, I do hear you."
Deep called to deep, now He's in charge again!

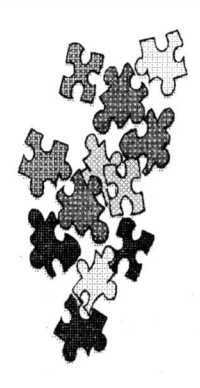

A Question of Worth

What would you give for the life of a child?
What is a child's life worth?
I do not speak of third world children,
Who die from hunger and thirst.

I speak of America, the land of the free,
Where none should be hungry or ill.
Where women can snuff out the life of a child,
Just with the help of a pill.

When preschool children carry a gun,
"To scare off a bully," they say.
When children are lying dead in the streets,
Our first though is, "Who will pay?"

When a child with an arsenal of powerful guns,
Hides in the woods in a rage.
And we see people and blood all around,
We ask God to please turn the page.

(continued)

When parents' hearts are torn from their bodies,
And lives are destroyed by one.
Who do we blame? Society, in general,
Or one single child with a gun?

When streets are red with the blood of our youth,
We wonder, "How did this begin?"
When will someone stand up with the truth,
And say, "We're all a part of this sin."

God gave us these children as a blessing, not to abuse or allow to be abused. They are our tomorrows. Our church leaders, our business heads, the brain surgeons, our teachers and our fathers and mothers. When will Christian parents stand up together and form a tangible barrier between our kids and the destruction satan has in store for them? I believe that's our job!

Some Things I Need to Know

Dear Lord, I want so many things,
I don't know where to start.
I think the first thing that I need,
Is a brand new fleshly heart.

I want to be more like you, Lord.
I want to be less like me.
I cannot always trust me, Lord,
So I put my trust in thee.

So many things I want to do,
But Lord, what if I fail?
I need to know you'll be with me,
In every storm and gale.

I long to do so many things,
But Lord, I'm often weak.
The only time I'm A-okay,
Is if I hear you speak.

(continued)

The world is full of sinners,
And the lost ones must be found.
Just point the way and give me strength,
And please, Lord, don't let me down.

I want to feed the hungry, Lord.
I want to see sick healed.
By myself I can do nothing,
So to you I have appealed!

I go to work, there's much to do.
The pace is fast and hard.
And when I go to bed at night,
I'm often very tired.

So what is more important, Lord?
Just please show me the one.
Just give me strength from day to day.
I'm sure I'll get it done!

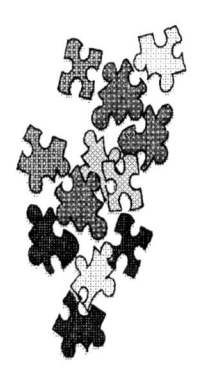

Remembering Michael

I remember the first time you came to my house.
You were only about three days old.
Your mom had you wrapped from head to toe,
And it wasn't too awfully cold.

Your mom sat down and unwrapped you, Mike,
With all of us gathered around.
I remember so well the small button nose,
And the eyes that were black, not brown.

You weren't the first baby we'd ever seen,
As I'd had some of my own.
But you did seem different in a strange way,
And you brought much joy to our home.

We set up your crib in the living room,
And began seeing life through your eyes.
You became so important we all found ourselves,
Straining our ears for your cries.

(continued)

You had such a presence it was felt right away.
It seemed to be there from the start.
And before we knew it we were firmly tied,
To you by the strings of our hearts.

Now you're growing up, Mike, and sometimes you're gone,
But your presence is felt just the same.
You're an integral part of who I am,
And without you it's just not the same.

We know you'll grow up and have your own life.
It was meant to be thus from the start.
But we know you'll come back for we'll draw you back,
By these deep cords of love in our hearts.

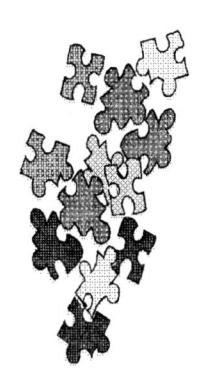

The Modern Raven

Once upon a midnight jivey,
All the cats were loud and lively,
As they listened to some jazzy, jivey, jumpy Presley tunes.
Dig that Elvis! Dig that tune!
Hep stuff straight from Tin Pan Alley,
Meat and drink for Sam and Sally.
Tho' this music to Beethoven faint resemblance ever bore.
Jive it was and nothing more.
Still they screamed and swooned and fainted,
As they fell upon the floor.

Suddenly the night was shattered,
By this time it scarcely mattered,
By the screeching, screaming, sobbing sound of tires upon the road.
How they held I've never knowed.
Then the Raven made his entrance,
Smiled and bowed and made his entrance,
Bearing in his hand a platter labeled Boon forevermore!
Boon records at a Presley party? Cats what are you waiting for?
Grab the Raven, kill the craven, make him holler evermore.

(continued)

All the cats fell on the Raven,
For his silly misbehavin'.
One guy grabbed him from behind,
And down they fell upon the floor.
In the nose he firmly poked him,
Grabbed him by the neck and choked him,
And in other way provoked him,
As they rolled upon the floor.
Rocked and rolled and puffed and panted,
As they wrestled on the floor.
Mayhem this and nothing more!
Such a sorry seeming Raven you have never seen before.

Forgive me Poe for what I'm doin',
This I know will be your ruin.
But the Raven had it coming,
So forgiveness I implore.
Squawks and squeaks from every section,
Feathers flew in all directions,
Imprecations and inflections from the Raven on the floor.
Finally he reached the doorway,
Staggered through and made the roadway.
Reached his car as all the cats came streaming through the door.
The motor coughed and sputtered,
Naughty words the Raven muttered,
And a few words that he uttered, I had never heard before.
But one thing he said plainly,
And the theme of it was mainly,
Attend another platter party?
OH, BROTHER! NEVERMORE!

Reprinted with permission by the author Bonita Johnston

A Lesson Well Learned
or
Please Don't Ever Co-sign

I need a car, man,
What can I say?
What I really had in mind
Was another Chevrolet.

The one I've got,
Is sixteen years old,
And that's a ripe old age,
For a car, I'm told.

I'm not complaining.
I still love my car.
But I'm afraid to go fast,
And scared to go far.

Once upon a time,
In my generosity,
I put my name on a line,
Where everyone could see.

(continued)

Co-sign they called it.
A trick's what I say.
And if I hadn't bought a Ford,
I could get a Chevrolet.

So now I'm in a mess, man.
I really am stuck.
But I'm trusting God
To get me out of this rut.

Now I'm done with my story.
That's all I've got to say.
But when I pay for this Ford,
I'm gonna get a Chevrolet!

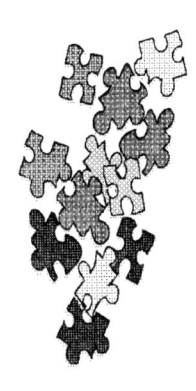

The Sadness in Colorado

With death and dying all around,
We place our kids beneath the sod.
Life's blood spilled upon the ground,
But through it all we still see God!

With fear and terror all around,
With futures dim or almost gone,
With boys and girls dead on the ground,
They still find strength to carry on.

They were so open with their faith.
They prayed with others, held their hand.
They prayed in each and every place,
Although they could not understand.

"How could this happen?" newsmen say.
"They seemed so normal," most folks said.
No one predicted such a day.
Can someone, please, explain the dead?

(continued)

What could be done? How did they fail?
"We tried so hard!" the people say.
We look for answers, yet we fail.
So look and pity us today.

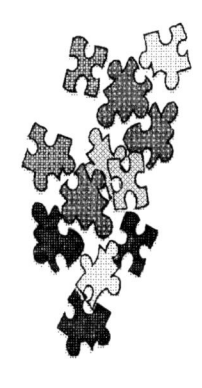

Surprise! Surprise!

I've had surprises all of my life,
Some good and some were bad.
The one I had on Wednesday, twelfth,
Was the greatest one I ever had.

My life's been one great controversy.
I never thought of myself as much.
I don't have a smooth exterior,
And I don't have that special touch.

I've never pushed myself forward,
Tho' I've wished many times I could read,
A poem or story that agreed with the pastor.
We all have our own special need.

I'm not a shy person, I'll try anything.
I guess I sort of like attention.
I've always wanted to do service for God,
Tho' I'm not called the mother of invention!

(continued)

So now I've been asked to do something to help.
I'm so humbled I hardly can speak.
I'm asked to serve for a year as a deacon,
And I really don't know how to deac!

Epimethius:
Something About Each of My Seven Children

And now, as I begin to finish this project, I'd like to say something about each of my children.

On May 16, 1947, Roy Francis Key Jr. was born. I learned many things from him. The first thing was the true feeling of love with all kinds of emotions added. I never knew love before him. There was love for parents, teachers, siblings and friends, but none of these compares to the love I felt for my son. Something very special came with this package. He became my whole life! I didn't spoil him. I wanted him to behave and know how to interact with other people. He is now fifty-three years old. He had only one child (no one knows why only one). Her name is Terry Lynn Key Abbott.

Roy is married to a great wife that I have loved since we first met. Her name is Kathy.

Roy is a certified mechanic, self-employed. He is still my first love. His daughter gave me my first great-grandchild, Nicholas Abbott. He is now five years old.

360/MY LIFE IN BITS 'N' PIECES

Roy, Kathy and Terry at her graduation

Roy, me and Terry at her graduation

361/MY LIFE IN BITS 'N' PIECES

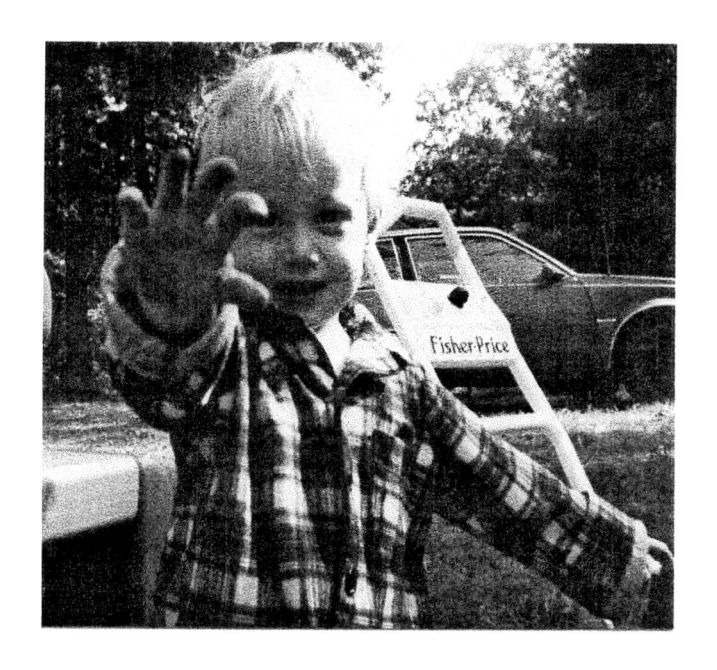

My first great-grandchild, Nick

Roy's first race car

On July 2, 1949, my second child arrived—the most beautiful little girl a mother could ever dream of. Her name is Regina Gail (Key) Raper, now fifty-one years old. The love factor did not shake me this time, because I had already experienced it. But it was no less the second time. She became my immediate life, just as the first one had.

She grew up well and healthy, never complained or demanded her way, a well-adjusted child. She married one of the greatest guys in the world. They have two children: Kellie Marie who has two boys, Damien Ray Waldo and Cameron Waldo; and Shannon Wayne Raper. Kellie is twenty years old and Shannon is eighteen.

Gina divorced her husband later. I never knew why. He and I are still the best of friends.

Alabama and Gina

363/MY LIFE IN BITS 'N' PIECES

Shannon

Kellie

Then on October 25, 1953, a second son was born. Here was a fine looking boy, who weighed in at nine pounds, six ounces. In this child I had beauty and the beast in one gorgeous package. The beauty caught everyone's attention early on. And the beast began to emerge later, especially after two more girls came along.

His name is Billy Jon Key, now forty-six years old. He was big and rough and something of a bully, and kept the girls agitated much of the time. But he did grow up and now has a personality one would die for. He is also a mechanic, very handy to have around.

He made a very bad marriage, had two children. Keri Jon is twenty-three years old, and Teah Marie is nineteen years old. Billy and his wife were divorced later, and he came home to live for a long time. We had his kids for a lot of that time.

Billy has two children by another girl. Dale is twenty-seven years old, and Rayanne is about six. They live in Arkansas.

Billy, me, Keri and Teah at Keri's graduation in 1995

365/MY LIFE IN BITS 'N' PIECES

Teah, Billy and Keri on Christmas day 1993

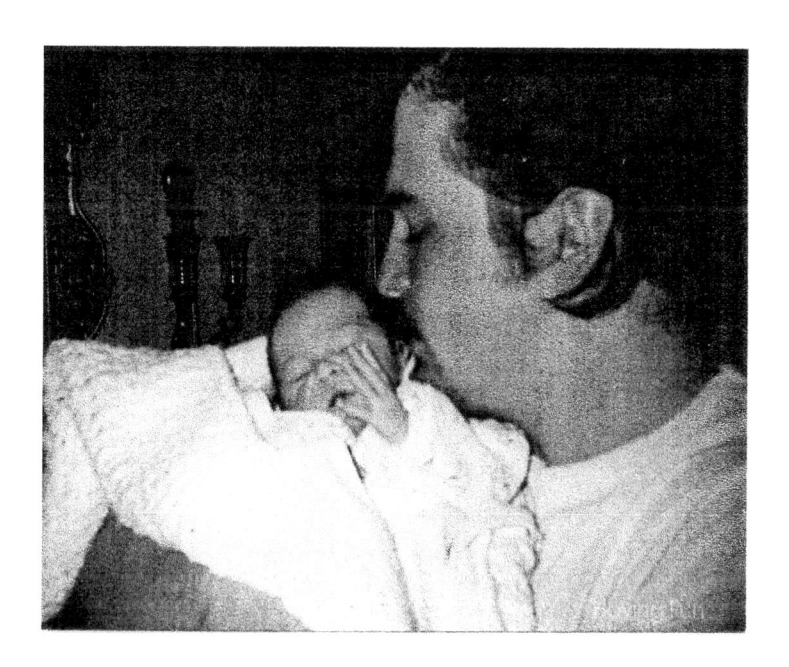

Rayanne Nicole and Dale Eugene

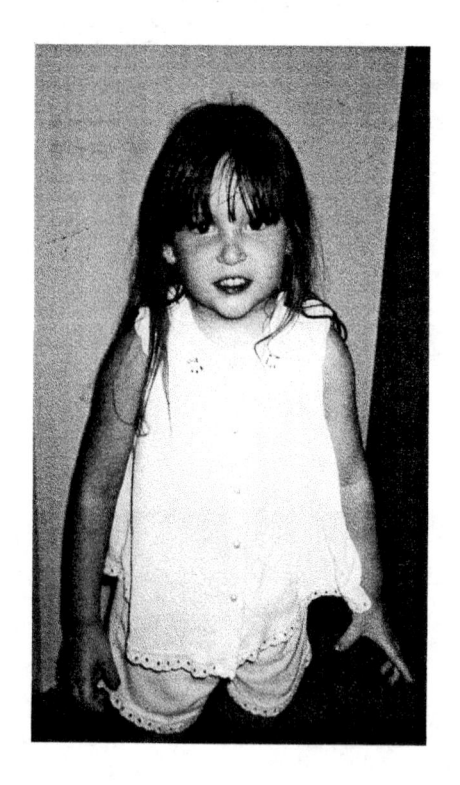

Rayanne

September 16, 1955, my family increased again. A lovely daughter was added. Starlyn Carol (Key) Stoup is now forty-five years old. She was never able to have children. She became a very fine seamstress, makes wedding ensembles and other equally hard-to-make items. She is very ambitious and would never settle for anything less than the best.

She married a great guy, John W. Stoup, a few years ago. He came from a totally different background than ours financially. They have flown me places and taken me to see things that I never would have been able to see or go to without them. And I'm very grateful. I'm very proud of her, and the love is still the same!

John and Star's wedding in "The Winner's Circle" at Saratoga Racetrack in New York

Then on May 22, 1957, comes a wild one, Lee Ann Holly (Key) Graves. She married a great guy also, very intelligent, Darrell D. Graves. They have two kids: Joey D., twenty years old; and Michelle, sixteen years old.

Holly has the personality that makes her the life of any gathering. She is sought after because she is so much fun. But she has a dark side too, a Gemini or a dual personality, if you will. But the good far outweighs the bad.

She still has close relationships with childhood friends, and that speaks much for her, I think.

She and her husband divorced years ago but have lived together and raised their kids. I don't understand this, but what can I say? All are different, but all loved the same.

Holly and Darrell

Joey and Michelle

And now, September 30, 1960, another girl child is born. This one is no better, but is very different. She did not marry the man, but had a ten-year "thing" and had two great boys. His name was Dale Ver Hey. Their first son's name is Michael Dale Ver Hey. He is now sixteen years old. Chad Allen Ver Hey is fourteen years old. I don't really understand this for I always thought, "First comes love. Then comes marriage. Then comes the mother thing and the baby carriage." But here she stands living proof that my theory doesn't always work!

She and I have a very different relationship. She's the rock I lean on. She was only six when her father died. I didn't start leaning until much later. But as I grow older, I find myself needing someone more often, and it seems to fall to Melodi to help me along. Melodi Rae is her name.

When she and Dale broke up she continued to live with me. I don't know what is in her future, but I hope it is happiness. She's not had much of that yet.

She does have a great job that she enjoys. She takes good care of the boys. Helps me a lot too.

December 17, 1998, she married a very fine man. They built a new house and things are going very well. And his name is Ken Post.

Melodi holding Chad and Michael

371/MY LIFE IN BITS 'N' PIECES

Michael Ver Hey

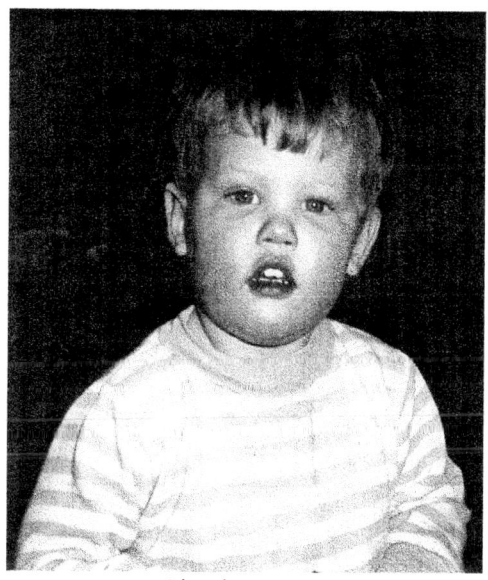

Chad Ver Hey

Melodi and her husband, Ken Post

And now, my last great love on January 21, 1964, was born. Another baby girl named Quaita Jahree (Key) Bridges. When she was six months old her father left for parts unknown. I never had to share her with anybody. She was my special joy. All mine! She is now thirty-five years old and married to a great guy. His name is Paul Bridges. They have two children: Ashley Ann Bridges, age sixteen years; and Joshua Paul Bridges, age thirteen.

I can truthfully say, Quaita never caused me to shed a single tear. I'm sure she is not perfect, but she's always been good.

My youngest daughter, Quaita, and her husband, Paul

Paul, Quaita, Joshua and Ashley

375/MY LIFE IN BITS 'N' PIECES

Ashley Bridges

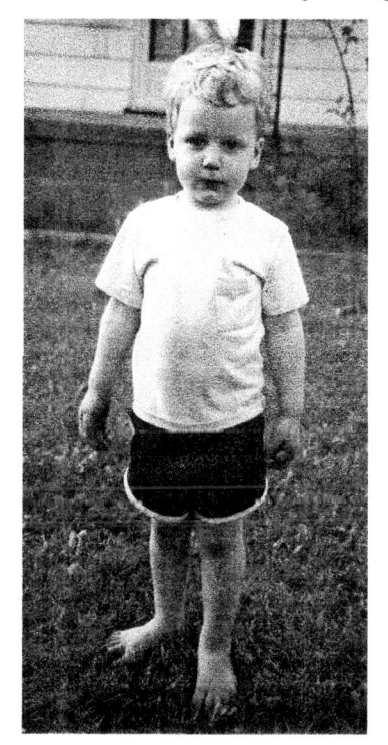

Joshua Bridges

When I look back and review some facts in my life, I'm amazed. I was never good-looking and my husband was no Clark Gable. So I'm left to wonder where did I get all these good-looking children? I guess it was from the same place where I got all my love from. It was all a gift from God!

Governor Millikin and me on Mackinaw Island in 1976

If you enjoyed this book, or any other book from Koenisha Publications, let us know. Visit our website or drop us a line at:

>Koenisha Publications
>3196 – 53rd Street
>Hamilton, MI 49419
>Phone or Fax: 616-751-4100
>Email: koenisha@macatawa.org
>Website: www.koenisha.com

Koenisha Publications authors are available for speaking engagements and book signings. Send for arrangements and schedule or visit our website.

Purchase additional copies of this book from your local bookstore or visit our website.

>Send for a free catalog of titles from Koenisha Publications.